Up and Running on Microsoft Viva Connections

Engage, Inform, and Empower Your Hybrid Workforce

Nanddeep Sadanand Nachan
Smita Sadanand Nachan

Apress®

Up and Running on Microsoft Viva Connections: Engage, Inform, and Empower Your Hybrid Workforce

Nanddeep Sadanand Nachan
Pune, Maharashtra, India

Smita Sadanand Nachan
Pune, Maharashtra, India

ISBN-13 (pbk): 978-1-4842-8605-0
https://doi.org/10.1007/978-1-4842-8606-7

ISBN-13 (electronic): 978-1-4842-8606-7

Managing Director, Apress Media LLC: Welmoed Spahr
Acquisitions Editor: Smriti Srivastava
Development Editor: Laura Berendson
Coordinating Editor: Shrikant Vishwakarma
Copy Editor: Kim Wimpsett

Cover designed by eStudioCalamar

Cover image designed by Freepik (www.freepik.com)

Distributed to the book trade worldwide by Springer Science+Business Media New York, 1 New York Plaza, Suite 4600, New York, NY 10004-1562, USA. Phone 1-800-SPRINGER, fax (201) 348-4505, e-mail orders-ny@ springer-sbm.com, or visit www.springeronline.com. Apress Media, LLC is a California LLC and the sole member (owner) is Springer Science + Business Media Finance Inc (SSBM Finance Inc). SSBM Finance Inc is a **Delaware** corporation.

For information on translations, please e-mail booktranslations@springernature.com; for reprint, paperback, or audio rights, please e-mail bookpermissions@springernature.com.

Apress titles may be purchased in bulk for academic, corporate, or promotional use. eBook versions and licenses are also available for most titles. For more information, reference our Print and eBook Bulk Sales web page at www.apress.com/bulk-sales.

Any source code or other supplementary material referenced by the author in this book is available to readers on GitHub (https://github.com/Apress). For more detailed information, please visit www.apress. com/source-code.

Printed on acid-free paper

Dedicated to our parents,
Shri Sadanand Nachan and Mrs. Archana Nachan.
—Smita Sadanand Nachan

My wife,
Mrs. Sarika Nanddeep Nachan,
and
our lovely son, Aditya Nanddeep Nachan.
—Nanddeep Sadanand Nachan

Table of Contents

About the Authors.. xiii

About the Technical Reviewer xv

Acknowledgments xvii

Introduction xix

Chapter 1: Microsoft Viva for Everyone 1

Hybrid Working Model.. 1

Benefits of Hybrid Working 2

Challenges of Hybrid Working.. 3

Employee Experience Platform 4

Microsoft Viva: Microsoft's New EXP... 5

Microsoft Viva Modules.. 5

Microsoft Viva Connections 5

Microsoft Viva Insights 6

Microsoft Viva Topics 7

Microsoft Viva Learning... 9

Viva Goals 10

Viva Sales 10

Licensing Model for Microsoft Viva 10

Conclusion 10

Chapter 2: Microsoft Viva Connections Capabilities and Setup Prerequisites 11

A Modern Employee Experience 11

Viva Connections Desktop Experience 12

Dashboard 13

Global Navigation... 14

Intranet Experience 14

Search Within the Intranet 15

Share Content 15

Feed for Viva Connections 15

Viva Connections Mobile Experience 17

Dashboard 17

Feed 18

Resources 19

Curated and Tailored Experiences 19

Curated Experience 20

Tailored Experience 20

Branding 20

Localization 20

Enable Multilingual Experience in SharePoint 21

Setting Up Viva Connections 21

Step 1: Prepare Your Intranet 21

Step 2: Set Up a Home Site 22

Step 3: Enable the App Bar and Global Navigation 22

Step 4: Create a Dashboard and Cards 22

Step 5: Prepare Content for the Feed 23

Step 6: Add the App to Teams 23

Step 7: Choose Mobile Settings 23

Step 8: Launch with End Users 24

Conclusion 24

Chapter 3: Prepare Your SharePoint Intranet **25**

The Role of an Intranet in an Organization 25

Modern SharePoint Experience 26

Information Architecture 26

Navigation 27

Branding 28

Template Support 28

Search 29

Collaboration 29

Performance 29

Multilingual 29

Flat Hierarchy 29

Hub Sites 30

Migrate from Classic to Modern SharePoint 32

Enable Modern User Experience on Lists and Libraries 32

Connect a Site to a Microsoft 365 Group 32

Modernize Classic Pages 32

Conclusion 33

Chapter 4: Home Site Superpowers 35

Plan for the Home Site 35

Stakeholder Engagement 37

Enable Engaging Employee Experience 38

Plan for Navigation 38

Personalize the Content 38

Monitor the Performance 38

Home Site Superpowers 38

Official Source of News 39

Home Site Features 39

Build the Home Site 40

Set Up a SharePoint Site 41

SharePoint Lookbook 43

Set the Site as the Home Site 44

Launch a Home Site 46

Make a Home Site Available to Everyone 46

Monitor the Home Site Performance 46

Schedule the Site Launch 48

Track the Home Site Usage 52

Home Site vs. Root Site..54

    Root Site 54

    Home Site 54

Best Practices for the Home Site 54

Conclusion 55

Chapter 5: App Bar and Global Navigation 57

App Bar 57

Global Navigation 59

    Prerequisites 60

    Set Up Global Navigation 60

    Configure the Global Navigation 61

    Multilingual Support for Global Navigation..65

    Governance for Global Navigation 66

My Sites 67

My News 67

My Files..68

My Lists..69

Temporarily Disabling the SharePoint App Bar 70

Quick Tips for the App Bar..71

Role of the App Bar in Viva Connections 71

Conclusion 72

Chapter 6: Authoring the Dashboard and Cards 73

Basics of the Dashboard 73

    Dashboard Mobile Experience..74

    Dashboard Desktop Experience..75

Dashboard Exploration...75

Define Your Dashboard...76

Multilingual Support for Dashboard 77

Add Cards to the Dashboard 78

    Mobile View 79

Desktop View 79

Add a Card 79

Web Link Card 80

Assigned Tasks Card 82

Teams App Card 84

Shifts Card 85

Approvals Card 86

Top News Card 87

Card Designer Card 87

Preview and Publish Dashboard 92

Partner Solutions 93

Access and Install the Partner Solutions 94

Custom Development 95

Employee Dashboard Example with Cards 95

Employee Engagement 96

Facilities 97

IT Support 97

Pay and Benefits 97

Conclusion 98

Chapter 7: Define Your Content Feeds **99**

Basics of Feeds 99

User Experience for Feeds 100

Sources of Content Feeds 103

User Experience for a Content Refresh 105

Content Ranking 105

User Actions on Feed 106

Role of Content Creator 106

Feeds from SharePoint 107

Organizational News Site 107

Designate a SharePoint Site as an Organizational News Site 107

Bring the News Experience to Users 108

News Boost Feature 111

Insights and Analysis.. 112

Yammer... 114

Feature a Conversation.. 115

Deploy the Communities App... 116

Insights and Analysis.. 117

Microsoft Stream (Built on SharePoint).. 120

Microsoft Stream (Classic) 120

Microsoft Stream (Built on SharePoint) 121

Migrating to Microsoft Stream (Built on SharePoint) 121

Video News Links... 121

Step 1: Create a Sharing Link 121

Step 2: Publish the Video as a News Item 122

Conclusion 125

Chapter 8: Enable Viva Connections in Microsoft Teams....................... 127

Understanding the Process.. 127

Permissions.. 128

Enable the Viva Connections App in the Teams Admin Center 128

PowerShell for Desktop-Only Experience... 128

Enable the Viva Connections App for Both Desktop and Mobile Users 132

Customize the App Settings 134

Details Section.. 134

Icons Section 136

Define Policies for the App.. 137

Defining Your Rings for a Phased Rollout 138

Define Permission Policies 138

Assign Permission Policy to Users 140

Manage Permission Policies with PowerShell... 143

Assigning a Permission Policy to the Groups 144

Points to Consider 145

Make the App Available to End Users...145

Define the App Setup Policy 146

Install the App..147

Pin the App to the Teams App Bar 147

Assigning a Setup Policy to Users 149

Assign a Setup Policy to Groups...150

Points to Consider 152

Viva Connections App in Action...152

Conclusion 153

Chapter 9: Define Mobile Settings for Viva Connections 155

Viva Connections Mobile Experience 155

Dashboard 155

Feed...155

Resources...155

Dashboard for Viva Connections Mobile Experience...........................156

Define Settings for the Mobile App 158

Conclusion 158

Chapter 10: Define End-User Guidance...159

End-User Psychology 159

How Easy or Difficult Is It?..159

Prepare Your Adoption Plan...160

User Engagement 160

Spread Awareness..161

Training..161

Measure the Success 162

Conclusion 163

Chapter 11: Extending Viva Connections..165

The Need for Extensibility 165

Extensibility Options with SPFx...166

Tools and Libraries for SPFx 167

Extensibility with Web Parts..168

Extensibility with Application Customizers 169

Extensibility with Adaptive Card Extensions 169

    Scaffold SPFx Solution for ACE 170

    ACE Class (Base Class)...171

    Card View...172

    Quick View 173

    Deploy the Solution 175

Conclusion 176

Chapter 12: Set Up a Governance Strategy................................177

The Need for Governance...177

Governance for a SharePoint Intranet...178

    Vision 179

    Information Architecture..179

    Policies 180

    Site Creation..180

    Navigation and Search 180

    Branding 180

    Custom Development and Deployment 182

    Feedback 182

    Training..182

    Measure the Success 183

    Governance Checklist for Home Site 183

Stay on Top of Changes...183

    Microsoft 365 Roadmap 184

    Message Center in Microsoft 365...185

Conclusion 185

Index...187

About the Authors

Nanddeep Sadanand Nachan is a three-time Microsoft MVP (M365 Apps & Services), and a Microsoft Certified Trainer. He is a results-oriented technology architect with experience in Microsoft technologies, especially with Microsoft 365, SharePoint, MS Azure, and Power Platform. He is experienced in the design, implementation, configuration, and maintenance of large-scale projects. He focuses on architectural design and implementation, website design and development, and complete application development cycles, with an intense focus on .NET technologies. He is an active contributor to the PnP Microsoft 365 Platform Community.

Smita Sadanand Nachan Her accolades include being a two-times Microsoft MVP in the M365 development category, a Microsoft certified trainer and author. Smita's book on Understanding Hybrid Environments in SharePoint was published by Apress publisher. She has 14+ years' experience in Microsoft technologies, especially with Microsoft 365 including SharePoint, MS Teams, Power Platform, Groups, Yammer and Forms. She like to interact with the people. She believes in sharing is caring and to live that she organizes as well as speak at various community events including SPS, Global Microsoft 365 Developer Bootcamp, and Global Power Platform Bootcamp. She is an active contributor to the Microsoft 365 community (`http://aka.ms/m365pnp`). In her personal life, Smita is a keen Instagram blogger with more than 12,000 followers. Her passions include photography, travel, fashion and being a mehndi artist.

About the Technical Reviewer

Waldek Mastykarz is a cloud developer advocate at Microsoft focusing on Microsoft 365. In this role, he helps developers build applications on top of Microsoft 365. He's also part of the Microsoft 365 platform community where he builds developer guidance and tooling for extending Microsoft 365 together with the community.

Before joining Microsoft, Waldek worked with different Microsoft partners in the Microsoft 365 space. For sharing his experience through his blog, speaking, and social media, Waldek was a 12-time Microsoft MVP.

Acknowledgments

I want to acknowledge that without my coauthor Miss Smita Nachan's initiative and zeal, this book would have not progressed beyond the idea stage.

I would like to thank everyone at Apress for giving us this opportunity to publish our book.

I would like to thank my parents for their endless support and for helping us in numerous ways. I would also like to thank my loving and caring wife, Mrs. Sarika Nachan, and my dear son, Aditya, who supported and encouraged me despite all the time it took me away from them. Both of them should get equal credit for bringing this book to fruition.

I would also like to thank the technical reviewer, Mr. Waldek Mastykarz, for his vigilant reviews, suggestions, corrections, and expert opinions.

—Nanddeep Sadanand Nachan

Writing this book was a beautiful journey that I am glad I took. The journey spanned a few months; however, the experience will last a lifetime.

I am extremely grateful to my parents, Mrs. Archana Sadanand Nachan and Mr. Sadanand Govind Nachan, for their love, prayers, and care, as well as for preparing me for the future. Special thanks to my brother, Nanddeep Nachan, for guiding me through this entire journey from writing content to converting it into a valuable book. The completion of this book could not have been accomplished without the support of my family.

Finally, I want to thank the Apress team, especially those who helped us to complete this book, our second with Apress.

—Smita Sadanand Nachan

Introduction

Most of us have been working in a remote or hybrid mode for the past couple of years during the global pandemic. Hybrid work is the present and future. Across all industrial areas, many organizations have adopted the hybrid way of working.

Hybrid work brings its own challenges for both organizations and employees. Team members can feel disconnected from their colleagues and managers. Managers and leads can lack engagement with their team. At the same time, organizations strive for smoother functioning by removing these obstacles and leveraging existing toolsets, without a need for additional tools.

Hybrid work requires new tools for employees and organizations to succeed. Microsoft provides a solution to these challenges with its new employee experience platform (EXP), Microsoft Viva.

For organizations to thrive and achieve more, Microsoft Viva offers various modules, namely, Viva Connections, Viva Insights, Viva Learning, Viva Topics, Viva Goals, and Viva Sales. There will be new modules added to the Microsoft Viva suite in the future.

Who This Book Is For?

This book is targeted at Microsoft professionals and business users who want to leverage the collaboration capabilities of Microsoft Viva Connections as an EXP to build a gateway to their digital workplace. The book will help you set up Microsoft Viva Connections for your digital workplace by providing easy-to-follow steps and show how to extend it to target your business scenarios.

How This Book Is Organized

This book is divided into 12 chapters, and it provides a detailed description of the various aspects of Viva Connections. Each chapter in the book begins with an explanation of the appropriate foundational concepts followed by a practical implementation to reinforce the explanation. A brief description of each chapter is as follows:

- *Chapter 1: Microsoft Viva for Everyone*: This chapter is an overview of Microsoft Viva and hybrid working concepts and is the foundation for the entire book. In this chapter, you are introduced to Microsoft Viva, including its modules, its significance, and how an organization can benefit from implementing it.

- *Chapter 2: Microsoft Viva Connections Experience Capabilities and Setup Prerequisites*: This chapter walks you through the Microsoft Viva Connections experience for desktop and mobile users. Also, we will cover the setup prerequisites for Microsoft Viva Connections.

- *Chapter 3: Prepare Your SharePoint Intranet*: This chapter provides the fundamentals of building an engaging intranet with SharePoint for the organization.

- *Chapter 4: Home Site Superpowers*: This chapter focuses on the key concepts of planning, building, and launching a SharePoint home site. It covers understanding the home site superpowers, exploring the SharePoint templates for the home site, and learning best practices for building a home site.

- *Chapter 5: App Bar and Global Navigation*: This chapter highlights the concept and importance of app bar and global navigation. Also, we will explore their roles in Viva Connections.

- *Chapter 6: Authoring Dashboards and Cards*: This chapter describes the concept and importance of dashboards and cards. Also, we will explore their role in Viva Connections.

- *Chapter 7: Define Your Content Feeds*: This chapter covers the different ways in which organizations can publish content that appears in the Viva Connections feed and how organizations can get the most out of the feed by combining the different types of content.

- *Chapter 8: Enable Viva Connections in Microsoft Teams*: This chapter discusses the process to configure the Viva Connections app in Microsoft Teams and defines a rollout strategy.

- *Chapter 9: Define Mobile Settings for the Viva Connections App*: To meet the usability expectations of both information workers and frontline workers, it is important to define the mobile settings for the Viva Connections app. This chapter gives guidance for the Viva Connections mobile settings.

- *Chapter 10: Define End-User Guidance*: This chapter explains how to make end users comfortable with this new offering and help them quickly adapt to Viva Connections.

- *Chapter 11: Extend Viva Connections*: This chapter covers how to extend Viva Connections with the SharePoint Framework (SPFx) to meet custom business scenarios. This chapter assumes prior experience with SPFx.

- *Chapter 12: Set Up a Governance Strategy*: This chapter focuses on the importance of defining governance for Viva Connections and how it helps an organization stay compliant with the processes and regulations.

CHAPTER 1

Microsoft Viva for Everyone

The world was running relatively smoothly until the pandemic hit and forced everyone to work remotely.

By necessity, many of us have been working in a remote or hybrid mode for the last couple of years, and it's shown us that hybrid work is the future. Across all industrial areas, various organizations have adopted the hybrid way of working.

In this chapter, you will be introduced to Microsoft's new employee experience platform (EXP), called Microsoft Viva, including its modules, its significance, and how an organization can benefit from implementing it.

Note Microsoft Viva leverages existing capabilities from Microsoft 365 including SharePoint, Teams, and Yammer. It is part of the Microsoft 365 suite.

Hybrid Working Model

The term *hybrid work* will be used throughout this book. So, let's start by discussing what the term means.

In a nutshell, a hybrid is something made by combining two different elements. Let's extend this definition to a working model with those two different elements being on-site and off-site working (Figure 1-1).

© Nanddeep Sadanand Nachan and Smita Sadanand Nachan 2022
N. S. Nachan and S. S. Nachan, *Up and Running on Microsoft Viva Connections*,
https://doi.org/10.1007/978-1-4842-8606-7_1

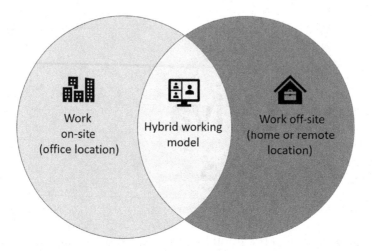

Figure 1-1. *Hybrid working model*

The hybrid working model brings location flexibility, which offers a choice for employees to work on-site (an office location) or off-site (a home or remote location) based on what an employee and their organization think is appropriate, productive, and convenient for them.

Benefits of Hybrid Working

The hybrid working model offers various benefits including the following:

- *Flexible working hours*: In the hybrid working model, employees have the flexibility to get their work done based on flexible hours instead of predefined office work hours and can stretch out their days to adjust to other time zones.

- *Better work-life balance*: With a hybrid working model, employees can define their own work schedule and fulfill both their personal and professional work obligations.

- *Ability to attract global talent*: Organizations can build a remote team of talented people with specialized skills to create better balanced teams. This allows organizations to attract global talent and retain the capabilities that support their business needs.

There is another side of this coin too: the challenges that come with a hybrid working model.

Challenges of Hybrid Working

Hybrid work brings its own challenges for both organizations and employees in terms of lack of engagement and communication. Microsoft Viva, a new employee experience platform, is the offering from Microsoft that helps you to overcome these challenges.

- *Disconnected feeling*: Interactions over virtual meetings are limited. As a result, individuals can feel disconnected from their fellow team members and managers. The human angle of sharing ideas and brainstorming solutions is very much limited in virtual meetings compared to face-to-face meetings.

  The Viva Connections module surfaces this problem by bringing relevant content in the form of news and conversations closer to users, who can carry out discussions and stay engaged with colleagues.

- *Keep up-to-date with learning*: In a hybrid working model, sharing thoughts and knowledge with team members is a bit difficult. Employees feel challenged to keep up-to-date with technology and the latest happenings. Learning with peers is considered the most effective option, which does not work best in virtual mode.

  The Viva Learning module addresses this by making learning part of everyone's daily life. The learning resources from various sources (e.g., Microsoft Learn modules, LinkedIn learning, third-party learning providers, and custom organization learning resources) help everyone learn at their own pace and grow. Everyone can learn together by sharing the content and recommendations.

- *Lack of team engagement for leaders*: Managers and leaders lack engagement with their teams in a virtual environment. Keeping the entire team synchronized is always challenging in a hybrid environment. Keeping track of everyone's work is difficult. When the employees have a disconnected feeling, it is challenging for the leaders to set up a nice employee experience. Leaders need to fill this gap by furnishing employees with the right skills and tools.

The Viva Insights module helps individuals, leaders, and managers be productive and improve their well-being. These insights will help you understand how well you are connected with your colleagues and leaders. The manager insights help them to understand employee burnout and to take corrective actions.

- *Organization challenges for smoother functionality*: At the same time, organizations strive for smoother functioning by removing these obstacles by leveraging existing toolsets without a need for additional tools.

Microsoft Viva is part of the Microsoft 365 suite. This makes it easy for organizations to adopt Microsoft Viva without any additional infrastructure and skillset investment.

Employee Experience Platform

EXP in simple words is a digital platform that organizations can implement to help their employees get involved, focus on their productivity and well-being, achieve their goals, and create a better work-life balance.

The following questions will help you design an EXP for your organization:

- How has hybrid working changed the organization's culture?

- How are you planning to bring the content closer to your employees?

- Do you have an existing communication channel set up to publish news and announcements for employees?

- How is the employee engagement on those communication channels?

- Do you have a feedback channel set up for your employees?

- How do you encourage ideas and feedback from your employees?

- How are you planning to achieve your organization's goals, mission, and vision by enabling an EXP?

Microsoft Viva: Microsoft's New EXP

As organizations adapt to the new hybrid working model and begin reopening their physical office locations, it's essential they rethink old paradigms and view their employees as being at the center of this new experience. Hybrid working brings a shift of focus for everyone including organizations, employees, culture, and technology.

When organizations invest in better employee experiences, they get beneficial returns in terms of retention, employee engagement, productivity, and customer satisfaction. Hybrid work requires modern tools for the employees and organizations to succeed. Microsoft's solution to these challenges is Microsoft Viva.

Organizations can reimagine the employee experience with Microsoft Viva. Microsoft Viva brings together everyone by enabling effective communications and helping to share knowledge, learn and grow together as a team, find resources, and carry out insights.

Today millions of users use Microsoft Teams daily for better engagement with colleagues and partners. It is a hub to bring together all resources and applications. Microsoft Viva extends this foundation by adding an employee engagement feature on top of it.

Microsoft Viva consists of various modules to offer these capabilities to users.

Microsoft Viva Modules

For organizations to thrive, Microsoft Viva offers various modules as of today: Viva Connections, Viva Insights, Viva Learning, Viva Topics, Viva Goals, and Viva Sales.

Now, we'll provide an overview of the existing Viva modules.

Microsoft Viva Connections

Microsoft Viva Connections is referred to as a gateway to a modern employee engagement experience.

Viva Connections helps to keep employees engaged and well informed. Microsoft 365 helps organizations to set up their modern digital workplace for better collaboration with various apps and services. Microsoft Teams is at the center of it. Microsoft is encouraging use of Microsoft Teams so that all the resources will be available to employees in one place. Figure 1-2 shows an example of a Microsoft Viva Connections app in Microsoft Teams.

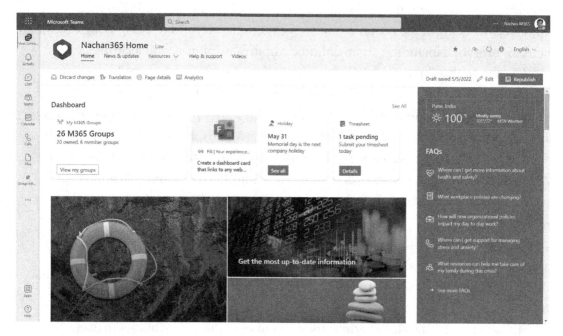

Figure 1-2. *Microsoft Viva Connections*

Viva Connections is based on the same theme as Microsoft Teams where, and employees will have all organizational updates in one place. These updates include news and announcements from SharePoint, conversations from Yammer communities, and videos from Stream.

In simple terms, Viva Connections surfaces the SharePoint home site in Microsoft Teams to provide a seamless experience to the users so that they can get the updates without leaving the Microsoft Teams interface.

Microsoft Viva Connections has mobile and desktop versions to meet the needs of information workers and frontline workers.

Microsoft Viva Insights

The Microsoft Viva Insights module is built on top of Workplace Analytics. It provides insights on user activities and suggestions to improve employees' well-being.

Figure 1-3 shows an example of the Microsoft Viva Insights experience in Microsoft Teams.

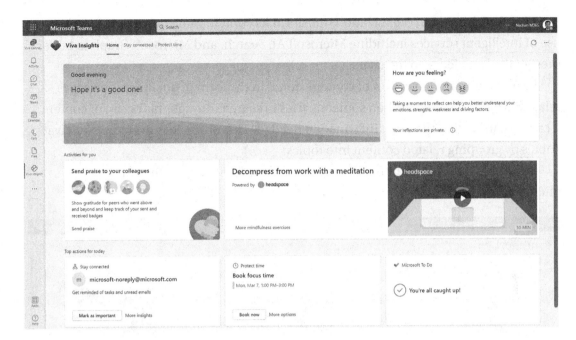

Figure 1-3. *Microsoft Viva Insights*

Viva Insights offers the following capabilities:

- *Personal insights*: By analyzing your working habits and patterns, it helps you to understand how you can perform better.

- *Manager insights*: It helps managers and team leaders understand and organize teamwork to help team members manage work-life balance.

- *Leader insights*: It analyzes employee engagement and adds value to an organization from the work culture point of view.

- *Advanced insights*: It helps to understand important aspects of the business by identifying workload balance and business requirements.

- *Data privacy*: It helps you to keep your personal data secure.

Microsoft Viva Topics

Microsoft Viva Topics helps organizations to transform their information into knowledge.

Viva Topics helps an organization transform its content into knowledge. It makes use of intelligent services including Microsoft AI, Search, and Microsoft Graph to better present the knowledge to the users.

Every organization has a lot of content stored in the form of documents or pages related to different topics. When someone tries to search through this ocean of content, it can be hard to find the exact information needed. This obstacle is overcome by Viva Topics by grouping related content into topics.

Figure 1-4 shows an example of a Microsoft Viva Topics experience in Microsoft Teams.

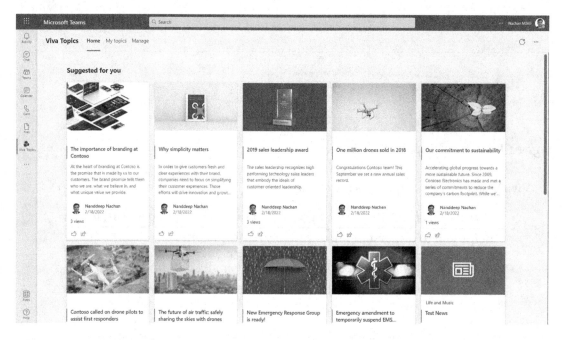

Figure 1-4. *Microsoft Viva Topics*

The topic results are displayed when users perform a search in SharePoint, Office. com, and Office applications (Word, PowerPoint, Outlook, and Excel). This knowledge indexing makes it easy to get relevant information on a topic defined by the organization.

For example, when someone searches for a project, product, event, or field of study, the topic helps users to understand it better with the following information:

- A short description

- Related people to further the discussion

- Files and sites related to the topic

Microsoft Viva Learning

Microsoft Viva Learning makes learning part of everyone's day.

Microsoft wants to promote a culture of learning, where learning will be an integral part of everyone's work life. Viva Learning enables everyone to learn, recommend, and share the content made available by the organization and partners without leaving the Microsoft Teams experience.

Figure 1-5 shows an example of a Microsoft Viva Learning experience in Microsoft Teams.

Figure 1-5. *Microsoft Viva Learning*

The learning sources include Microsoft Learn, Microsoft 365 Training, LinkedIn Learning, Go1, Skillsoft, Udemy, Edcast, and many other learning partners. Also, organizations can define their own learning sources by publishing learning videos on SharePoint and Stream.

Viva Goals

The new module of Microsoft Viva based on Ally.io is focused on objectives and key results. This will help employees define their goals and set objectives.

Viva Sales

The new module targeted to the sales experience allows sellers to use Microsoft 365 and Microsoft Teams to automatically capture the data in CRM systems.

Licensing Model for Microsoft Viva

With Microsoft 365 E3 or E5 licenses, you can access Microsoft Viva Connections at no additional cost. For the latest offerings, licensing, and cost details, visit `www.microsoft.com/en-us/microsoft-viva/pricing`.

Microsoft offers Microsoft Viva Suite at a lower price that includes Viva Learning, Viva Insights, Viva Topics, and Viva Goals.

Conclusion

Hybrid work is the future. Across all industrial areas, various organizations have adopted the hybrid way of working. Hybrid working brings with it challenges. Microsoft Viva, a new employee experience platform, is the answer to the challenges faced by employees, managers, leaders, and organizations. Microsoft Viva offers various modules, namely, Viva Connections, Viva Insights, Viva Learning, Viva Topics, Viva Goals, and Viva Sales.

In the next chapter, we will walk through the Microsoft Viva Connections experience for desktop and mobile users. Also, we will cover the setup prerequisites for Microsoft Viva Connections.

## CHAPTER 2

Microsoft Viva Connections Capabilities and Setup Prerequisites

Microsoft Viva Connections provides a curated employee experience. It surfaces relevant content such as news, announcements, communications, and conversations to employees. This makes the employee experience engaging and informative. It is an exciting time to reimagine the workplace as a digital experience rather than a physical place. This hybrid digital experience is people-centric, inclusive, and flexible.

In this chapter, you will understand the Microsoft Viva Connections experience for desktop and mobile users. Also, we will cover the setup prerequisites for Microsoft Viva Connections.

Note   Microsoft Viva Connections supports both mobile and desktop users.

A Modern Employee Experience

Viva Connections helps employees perform their work efficiently by staying up-to-date with important and relevant information without leaving Microsoft Teams. It brings together everything needed to work effectively including news, announcements, resources, apps, and tasks in the Microsoft Teams interface. Viva Connections helps strengthen relationships between individuals and their teams and helps leaders to improve the culture.

Viva Connections helps organizations utilize existing Microsoft 365 resources without any additional investments to modernize the employee experience.

© Nanddeep Sadanand Nachan and Smita Sadanand Nachan 2022
N. S. Nachan and S. S. Nachan, *Up and Running on Microsoft Viva Connections*,
https://doi.org/10.1007/978-1-4842-8606-7_2

This modern experience includes the following aspects:

- A single interface (i.e., Microsoft Teams) to stay updated with news, conversations, and tasks.

- A personalized experience to show relevant content to the employees, driven by AI and Microsoft Graph capabilities.

- A tailored experience by targeting the content to groups based on department, geography, etc.

- Organization branding matching your company's theme, color, and logo.

- The ability to utilize existing Microsoft 365 services to present the content from SharePoint news, Yammer conversations, and Microsoft Stream videos.

- The ability to leverage the underlying security and compliance features of Microsoft 365.

- The ability to bring in the experience of your partner offerings (like ServiceNow, Workday, etc.)

- The ability to extend Viva Connections by creating customized experiences with the SharePoint Framework (SPFx).

- The ability to support a wide range of users on desktop and mobile experiences.

Viva Connections Desktop Experience

For organizations on their journey to the cloud with Microsoft 365, SharePoint is the trusted choice to build their intranets. With SharePoint, authors can effectively create content in the form of news and announcements for better user engagement. The content can be targeted to a set of users to bring the content closer to them.

Microsoft Teams is at the center of the employee workplace; it not only is a chat-based workspace but goes beyond that and supports a digital workplace for organizations. Microsoft Teams brings in apps for every user need. Microsoft Viva Connections extends this concept to the surface by using a SharePoint home site as an app in Microsoft Teams. Viva Connections fosters an inclusive culture for both desktop and mobile users to meet the needs of information workers and frontline workers.

As employees start their day, in the past they needed to look in multiple places (e.g., SharePoint, Yammer, etc.) to get updates from the organization and their colleagues. They now have a place inside Microsoft Teams, which is the Viva Connections app, to get the updates in one place. In the desktop experience, Viva Connections is an app in Microsoft Teams to surface your organization's SharePoint home site in Microsoft Teams.

Figure 2-1 shows an example of the Microsoft Viva Connections experience in Microsoft Teams.

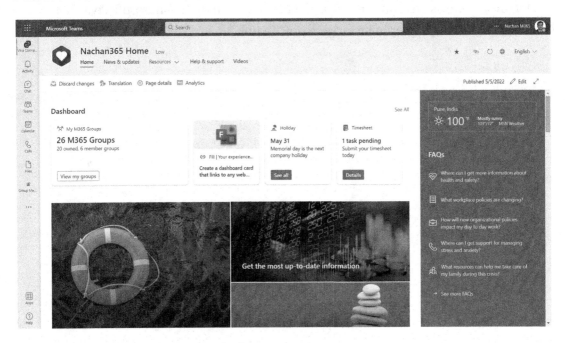

Figure 2-1. *Viva Connections desktop experience*

This figure highlights the Viva Connections desktop experience. The desktop experience has the following key elements.

Dashboard

The dashboard enables you to complete tasks and focus on important information. The dashboard is available on the home site, which displays *cards* for a better employee experience. Dynamic cards on the dashboard are authored in SharePoint and present relevant actions for users (e.g., track assigned tracks, view news, and engage in conversations).

Global Navigation

Global navigation presents users with a way to get to important resources curated for your organization. It helps you easily navigate to important sites, often visited locations, and leading organizational destinations.

Clicking the Viva Connections icon in the left navigation in Microsoft Teams will open the global navigation.

Figure 2-2 shows an example of the global navigation in the Microsoft Viva Connections desktop experience in Microsoft Teams.

Figure 2-2. *Viva Connections desktop experience, global navigation*

Intranet Experience

Viva Connections offers employees a consolidated experience to find everything they need during their working day. They do not need to visit multiple places like SharePoint, Yammer, etc., to get updates. The Viva Connections app in Microsoft Teams is a one-stop information shop for everyone.

Search Within the Intranet

Users can easily perform their searches from within Microsoft Teams with the Viva
Connections app. The Microsoft Teams search bar provides flexible search options.

Figure 2-3 shows an example of the search functionality in the Microsoft Viva
Connections desktop experience in Microsoft Teams.

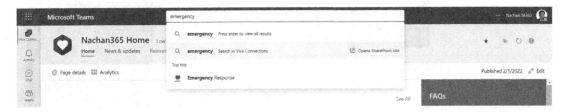

Figure 2-3. *Viva Connections desktop experience, search*

The "view all results" link shows the search results from Microsoft Teams.
The search in Viva Connections opens a SharePoint site with search results in a new
browser window.

Share Content

The intranet content can now be easily shared in Microsoft Teams for better
collaboration. The "Copy link" icon at the top of each page makes it easy to share the
content in a Teams chat.

Feed for Viva Connections

Feeds help you to discover and engage with news, announcements, and conversations.
The feed for Viva Connections is another web part that can be added to the SharePoint
home site.

Figure 2-4 shows an example of a feed for the Microsoft Viva Connections desktop
experience in Microsoft Teams.

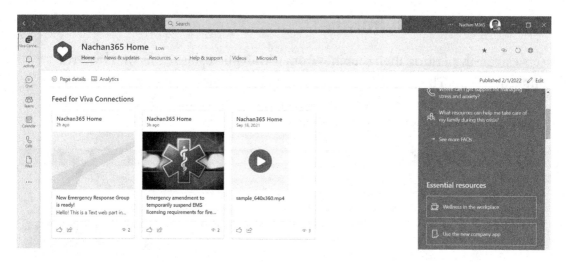

Figure 2-4. *Feed for Viva Connections*

The Feed for Viva Connections web part helps employees to stay up-to-date with conversations, news, and Stream videos. Employees can see this information based on the sites they follow.

The desktop experience also allows the users with specified permissions to create, update, and delete content from the SharePoint home site using the Viva Connections app.

Where Does the Content Come From in the Feed?

The content will be shown to the user depending on their access levels (as a user or as a member of a group). The content is surfaced from the following sources:

- *SharePoint*: The news from the home site, organizational news site, and sites you follow are shown.

- *Yammer*: Conversations from the All company community or communities you follow, as well as featured posts from public communities, are shown.

- *Stream*: Stream videos published as video news links or embedded in the news posts are shown.

Not all the content sources need to be configured. You can optionally choose to publish content for feeds from one or more sources.

Viva Connections Mobile Experience

The mobile experience for Viva Connections is optimized to focus on the dashboard, feed, and resources. Viva Connections was built to engage everyone including frontline workers who might not have access to the terminal at all times. A mobile experience can be very helpful to frontline workers by consolidating the shifts, tasks, news, poll participation, and discussions in one place.

Dashboard

The dashboard displays the dynamic cards to users to take quick actions.

Figure 2-5 shows an example of a dashboard with dynamic cards in the Microsoft Viva Connections mobile experience.

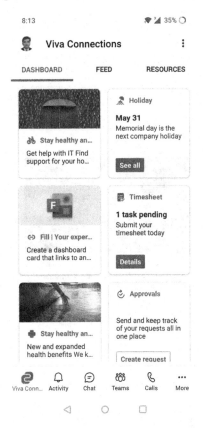

Figure 2-5. *Viva Connections mobile experience, dashboard*

The cards on the Viva Connections dashboard are based on adaptive cards. The SharePoint Framework (SPFx) provides a customization option to build your custom-tailored cards.

The SharePoint Framework is the choice of developers to extend modern SharePoint. It supports platform-agnostic, client-side development for SharePoint using modern web technologies and tools (e.g., Nodejs, npm, gulp.js, TypeScript, Yeoman, webpack, etc.). We will cover more about creating custom cards for the dashboard with SPFx in Chapter 11.

Feed

A feed can generally surface the content relevant to the user from SharePoint, Yammer, and Stream.

Figure 2-6 shows an example of a feed in the Microsoft Viva Connections mobile experience.

Figure 2-6. *Viva Connections mobile experience, feed*

Resources

The Resources section in the mobile experience displays the global navigation from SharePoint. It presents users with the navigation to important resources curated for their organization.

Figure 2-7 shows an example of global navigation named Resources in the Microsoft Viva Connections mobile experience.

Figure 2-7. *Viva Connections mobile experience, resources*

Curated and Tailored Experiences

Viva Connections presents options to create both curated and tailored experiences for content creators.

Curated Experience

The curated experience can be pushed to users by the site owner or authors. Site owners can use audience targeting to target content for users in Microsoft 365 groups and email-enabled security groups. They can target the content for dashboard items, menu items in global navigation, or content on the SharePoint home site.

The SharePoint home site, dashboard, and resources are examples of a curated experience.

Tailored Experience

In a tailored experience, the content is presented to users based on the communities or sites they follow in SharePoint, group membership in Yammer, or popular content.

A feed is an example of a tailored experience.

Branding

Every organization follows its own branding. This includes a logo and colors to show their brand. This Viva Connections app allows companies to apply organizational branding in Microsoft Teams.

We will cover more about branding in Chapter 8.

Localization

Viva Connections supports the major languages used across Microsoft 365. Viva Connections has major components, such as Dashboard, Feed, Resources, and the Teams mobile app, that constitute the Viva Connections experience.

- Dashboard authors can set the content to support multiple languages.

- SharePoint news in the feed will be displayed in the user's preferred language.

- Global navigation will follow the tenant's default language for Resources. At the same time, you can add localized text for menu items in the Global navigation per supported language.

Enable Multilingual Experience in SharePoint

For organizations operating in various regions, it is important to present the content in the user's native language. SharePoint supports multiple languages to satisfy this requirement. Start by creating your home site with English as a default language, enable the site to use multilingual features, and then choose the other languages the site will support.

We will cover more about multilingual features in Chapter 3.

Setting Up Viva Connections

Setting up Viva Connections requires business users to define what content to surface and the technical experts to design the architecture.

Figure 2-8 outlines the steps to follow for setting up Viva Connections experience.

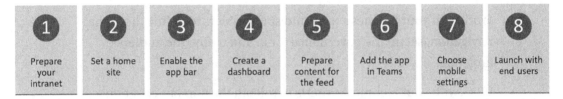

Figure 2-8. *Viva Connections setup steps*

We will go through the details of each step in the subsequent chapters. Each step is important and needs the involvement of multiple stakeholders including business users, service owners, technical experts, champions, etc.

Let's spend some time looking at the steps involved and understanding their significance from a business and technical point of view.

Step 1: Prepare Your Intranet

Get your SharePoint site ready to serve as a modern intranet for the organization.

- Work with your business users and stakeholders to figure out what is important to surface on the intranet for employees.

- Work with your technical experts to figure out how to design a performant intranet.

Step 2: Set Up a Home Site

The home site in SharePoint is your digital gateway for the employee experience and a prerequisite for Viva Connections.

- Work with your business users and stakeholders to define the layout of the home site, identify which content is important for employees, and determine how to present it to them.

- Work with your technical experts to design the information architecture for the home site.

Step 3: Enable the App Bar and Global Navigation

The app bar will surface important organization elements as well as personalized content to the employees.

- Work with your business users and stakeholders to define the global navigation, set up the governance for it, and define the audience targeting.

- Work with your technical experts to roll out the app bar experience.

Step 4: Create a Dashboard and Cards

The dashboard is the core of the Viva Connections experience, especially for the mobile experience. It helps to create a curated experience in the form of cards.

- Work with your business users and stakeholders to define the use cases for the dashboards, define which cards will be useful for employees, identify the partner solutions, and identify the need for developing custom cards.

- Work with your technical experts to author the cards on the dashboard, engage with partner solutions to onboard their cards on the dashboard, and develop custom cards with SharePoint Framework.

Step 5: Prepare Content for the Feed

The content is delivered to users from various sources or feeds including SharePoint, Yammer, and Stream. The feeds provide a tailored experience to users by presenting the most relevant content to them. To engage the end users, it is important to identify and bring the relevant content closer to them.

- Work with your business users and stakeholders to define the content sources, identify the content to feature, and set up the governance to publish the content.

- Work with your technical experts to define the information architecture and understand the capabilities in SharePoint and Yammer to empower Viva Connections.

Step 6: Add the App to Teams

After the content is defined, configure the Viva Connections app in Microsoft Teams and define a rollout strategy.

- Work with your business users and stakeholders to define the branding for the Viva Connections app and define a rollout strategy.

- Work with your technical experts to enable the app, define the permission, and set up policies to roll out the Viva Connections experience to the end users in a phased approach.

Step 7: Choose Mobile Settings

Design a better experience for information workers and frontline workers by meeting their usability expectations for a mobile experience.

- Work with your business users and stakeholders to optimize the mobile experience and define a card layout for the mobile dashboard experience.

- Work with your technical experts to make the app available to information workers and frontline workers.

Step 8: Launch with End Users

Define the end-user guidance to make them comfortable with this new offering and help them quickly adapt to Viva Connections.

- Work with your business users and stakeholders to prepare the adoption plan, build user engagement, spread awareness, and understand the training needs.

- Work with your technical experts to create forums to help employees on technical issues and measure success.

Conclusion

You now have a better understanding of the Microsoft Viva Connections experience for desktop and mobile users. We have briefed you on the setup process and prerequisites for Microsoft Viva Connections.

In the next chapter, we will start setting up Viva Connections by preparing our intranet in SharePoint.

CHAPTER 3

Prepare Your SharePoint Intranet

A modern SharePoint intranet is the key to the adoption and success of Microsoft Viva Connections. Many organizations have already been using the SharePoint platform to build engaging intranets. As Viva Connection surfaces the SharePoint home site inside Microsoft Teams, it is an important phase to plan your SharePoint intranet.

In this chapter, you will learn about the key concepts to building an engaging intranet with SharePoint for your organization.

The Role of an Intranet in an Organization

An intranet is home to key information across an organization. A digital workplace is a collection of tools that facilitate collaboration and communication, one of which is the intranet. It is an internal website that shares news and announcements. It serves as a platform to collaborate for employees. It reflects the culture of every organization. Therefore, an intranet should be considered a foundational element of your digital workplace. When designed and implemented corrrectly, it can play an important role in the work life of employees.

An intranet should not be a place to share read-only information that acts as one-way communication to employees. It should be a place where employees can express themselves by sharing their thoughts, inputs, and ideas to make the organization a better place to work.

© Nanddeep Sadanand Nachan and Smita Sadanand Nachan 2022
N. S. Nachan and S. S. Nachan, *Up and Running on Microsoft Viva Connections*,
https://doi.org/10.1007/978-1-4842-8606-7_3

Organization executives share important information on the intranet in the form of news posts, articles, discussions, etc. Every employee becomes part of it by sharing their thoughts via leaving comments, giving reactions, following topics, and sharing them with other colleagues. As a whole, an intranet is an integral part of every employee's day-to-day life.

Having an engaging intranet helps organizations to build a powerful culture for collaboration as well as adapt to newer challenges and changes to create better lives for themselves.

Modern SharePoint Experience

SharePoint is an offering from Microsoft 365 to build powerful intranets. SharePoint has a rich history of more than two decades serving as a platform for communication, collaboration, enterprise features, and much more.

With the following experiences, modern SharePoint helps developers build a robust and adaptive intranet for organizations.

Information Architecture

While building an intranet, having clarity on which content to surface makes it easy to define your information architecture.

Information architecture includes planning from the organization's intranet owners (e.g., service owners or product owners), department owners, IT admins, and individual site owners to define the following:

- What information should be surfaced on the site?

- Where do we surface the information?

- Which audiences are we targeting with the information?

- How do we best define the information hierarchy?

The following list highlights the involvement of each stakeholder at a given stage to implement information architecture for an organization:

- *Service owners and department owners* can define what and how they want to surface the information, as well as how to support any revisions based on user feedback after going live.

- *IT admins* can plan for the technical aspects to build the information architecture to make it robust and performant.

- *Content creators* can be involved at some later stage to make the content available to the employees and create a better presentation for the content.

Figure 3-1 shows a general plan and stakeholder involvement at various stages in the information architecture planning.

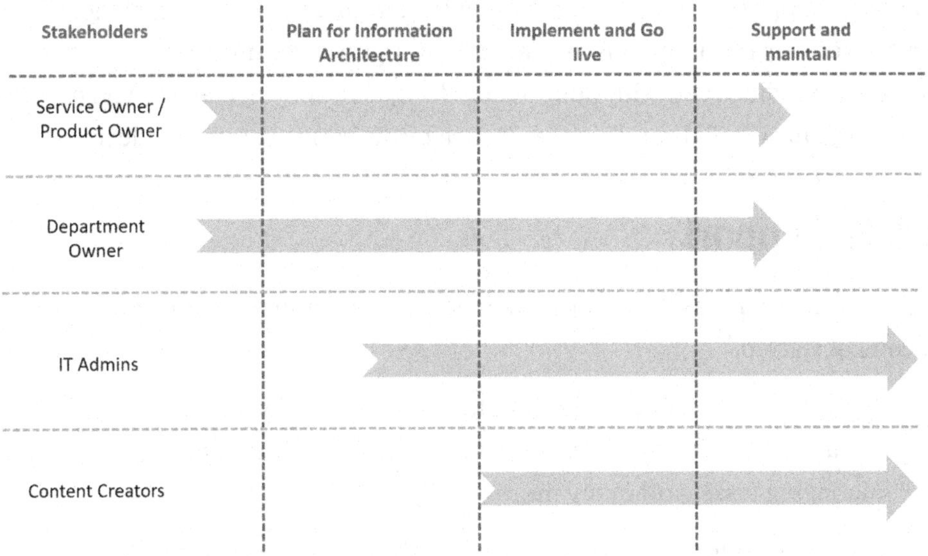

Figure 3-1. *Plan for information architecture*

Navigation

Well-thought-out navigation makes it easy for employees to quickly get to the information they are looking for. Hub sites play an important role in the navigation of content. Employees start their experience by browsing the content first before trying the robust search option.

Here are some tips for defining clear navigation:

- Group related links for navigation.

- Define clear labels for your navigation links.

- Define the correct placement for navigation links for better usability. Consider the global navigation and left navigation carefully.

- Define the visibility of links using audience targeting.

Branding

Presenting content based on your organization's look and feel is important. SharePoint offers theming support to brand your intranet by defining the colors and logo. This allows you to create a consistent look and feel throughout the intranet.

SharePoint provides you with built-in site designs to get you started. You can also create your organization's branding experience by defining custom site designs.

Template Support

SharePoint offers predefined templates like the team site and the communication site to help you get started.

- Team sites are useful to collaborate within a team by sharing documents, defining conversations, keeping track of events, managing tasks, and many more.

- Communication sites are used to publish dynamic, engaging content across the organization and keep everyone informed and engaged on topics, news, and events.

- The SharePoint lookbook is another option available from Microsoft to create great-looking sites quickly. The SharePoint lookbook templates can be accessed from `https://lookbook.microsoft.com`.

- Organizations can develop custom templates with site scripts and site design for common scenarios (for example, department based, location based, or functionality based, etc.).

Search

Search is the core of every intranet. Modern SharePoint search is personal as well as contextual. The results seen by every individual are unique to them based on their permissions and what they follow on an intranet.

Collaboration

SharePoint provides easy collaboration by sharing the content with colleagues. The collaboration can be within the organization, and with external sharing turned on, one can also share the content outside of the organization (e.g., with partners and vendors) for better collaboration.

Performance

The intranet is one of the busiest places in the organization. One can expect it to have heavy traffic all the time, considering all time zones in which the organization operates. Modern SharePoint is designed to be flexible and performant.

Multilingual

Content presented in a native language is easier for employees to read. Modern SharePoint supports multiple languages. A major element in the SharePoint intranet is that site navigation, site titles, and site descriptions are included in the multilingual support.

Modern SharePoint supports multiple languages by translated pages in a language-specific folder in the Site Pages library.

Flat Hierarchy

As we are adapting to modern SharePoint, we should think of the information architecture as a modern flat hierarchy over traditional or classic subsite hierarchy.

A flat hierarchy is based on the concept that every site is a site collection that can be represented as a discrete entity. Subsites are not recommended.

Microsoft promotes a flat site hierarchy with modern SharePoint. There are key benefits of adapting to a flat hierarchy. In a flat hierarchy, every site is a site collection with a unique responsibility.

If you think having a large number of site collections will make it difficult to connect them, then you can plan to use hub sites.

Hub Sites

Hub sites are one of the important building blocks of the SharePoint intranet. They are generally referred to as the "connective tissue" that binds related sites including team sites and communication sites.

With the flat hierarchy structure promoted by Microsoft, each unit of work should be a separate site collection.

Hub sites help to connect flat, structured site collections and have the following advantages:

- Common navigation

- Consistent branding (theme and logo) across all connected sites

- Search abilities within all connected sites

- Content from the connected sites on the hub site

In the past with classic SharePoint, organizations preferred an information architecture with a nested hierarchy structure, where multiple sites were placed under a root site. This approach was inflexible and involved designing the information architecture up front because the movement of any subsite later involved migration efforts as well as permission management.

Figure 3-2 shows an example of a nested hierarchy of SharePoint sites. Moving Sub Site A3 from Site Collection A to Site Collection B would involve the migration of data as well as permissions, which would need to be carried out as a separate migration project.

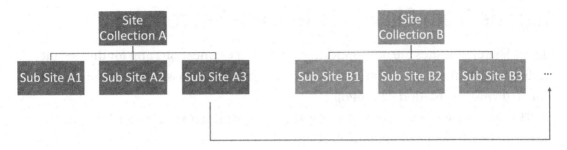

Figure 3-2. *Nested hierarchy*

A flat hierarchy, with every site being a separate site collection, offers the following benefits over the subsite information architecture.

Rearrange Site Structure

With a flat hierarchy, disassociating a site from one hub and associating it with another hub is an easy process.

Deletion of Site

With a nested hierarchy, deleting a site with subsites was difficult, if it had nested subsites below it. In a flat architecture, it is easy to delete sites without inadvertently removing any important content that you plan to keep.

Flexible Site Structure

With a flat architecture, it is easier to rearrange the site hierarchy without having to migrate anything.

Permissions Management

In a flat architecture, you no longer have to stop inheriting permissions and deal with complex permission models. Permission can be maintained at each site collection level.

External Sharing

In a nested hierarchy, external sharing could not be turned on for a single subsite but had to be on the site collection. In a flat architecture, this can be achieved easily without impacting other site collections.

Migrate from Classic to Modern SharePoint

Classic SharePoint sites are not supported in the Viva Connections app for the default landing experience in Microsoft Teams. If you are still using classic SharePoint, then it is time to upgrade to modern SharePoint.

The modern SharePoint experience is simple, flexible, and more user-friendly. Even if you have a huge number of classic SharePoint sites in your tenant, you can fully transform all of them into a modern experience with in-place modernization.

The experience in SharePoint is concentrated around the lists, libraries, and pages with which users interact most.

Enable Modern User Experience on Lists and Libraries

Consider using the SharePoint Modernization scanner available at `https://aka.ms/ sppnp-modernizationscanner` to detect the lists and libraries not following the modern experience.

To enable the modern experience in lists and libraries, consider replacing your JavaScript-based customizations and custom user actions with SharePoint Framework extensions for list views and columns. From the list and library settings, consider setting up a modern list experience.

Connect a Site to a Microsoft 365 Group

Modern SharePoint team sites are by default connected to Microsoft 365 groups, whereas classic SharePoint team sites are not. Connecting your SharePoint site to a Microsoft 365 group enables you to take advantage of group-connected services like Teams, Planner, Yammer, and Outlook.

Modernize Classic Pages

Transforming your classic pages to modern pages is an important step in modernizing your SharePoint site because users mostly deal with site pages. However, this process is not straightforward, because there is no straightforward mapping of classic to modern features.

Consider using PnP PowerShell (`https://aka.ms/pnp/powershell`) as a starting point to modernize your classic pages. At the same time, your customizations can be transformed with the SharePoint Framework (SPFx) web parts.

Conclusion

A modern SharePoint intranet is the key to setting up Microsoft Viva Connections. In this chapter, we briefed you on the key concepts of building an engaging intranet with SharePoint for your organization.

In the next chapter, we will take this a step further and show how to set up a home site and explain the intranet landing experience with the SharePoint home site.

CHAPTER 4

Home Site Superpowers

A home site is usually a SharePoint communication site that acts as the face of your organization's intranet. The home site surfaces news, conversations, pages, and discussions important to employees. The home site is a must if you are planning to have the Viva Connections experience in Microsoft Teams.

In this chapter, you will understand the key concepts to plan, build, and launch a home site; understand the home site's "super powers"; explore SharePoint templates for the home site; and learn best practices for building a home site.

Note After the Viva Connections app is deployed, your SharePoint home site will become a default landing experience in Microsoft Teams. However, if people open Microsoft Teams without going to Viva Connections, they will see chats, teams, or files rather than the home site.

Plan for the Home Site

A SharePoint home site is a primary prerequisite for setting up Viva Connections. It provides a landing experience for employees to reflect on the organization's brand, values, and culture. A home site can have global navigation, which helps to present important links to employees.

The home site can be an engaging experience for employees by doing the following:

- Surfacing attractive and dynamic content published for the enterprise from SharePoint

© Nanddeep Sadanand Nachan and Smita Sadanand Nachan 2022
N. S. Nachan and S. S. Nachan, *Up and Running on Microsoft Viva Connections*,
https://doi.org/10.1007/978-1-4842-8606-7_4

- Helping to engage with communities from Yammer and spark conversations

- Surfacing videos from Stream to communicate with colleagues through videos

Figure 4-1 shows the home page experience of the SharePoint home site.

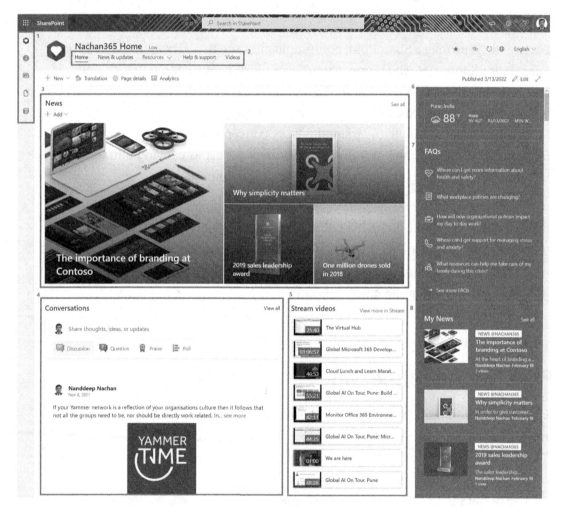

Figure 4-1.   *The home page of a SharePoint home site*

Figure 4-1 is an example of a home page in a SharePoint home site that surfaces information from various content sources in the following sections:

1. **SharePoint app bar**: Shows global navigation, My Sites, My News, My Files, and My Lists

2. **Local portal navigation**: Shows top navigation for the home site with links to important resources

3. **Featured News:** Image gallery of featured news articles of an organization

4. **Conversations:** Embedded Yammer conversations

5. **Videos:** Shows recommended videos from Stream

6. **Helpful resources:** Dynamic web part showing useful information

7. **Static links:** Static links to useful resources

8. **My News:** Dynamic personal news feed

The home site is not a type of site like a team site or communication site in SharePoint. Rather, any communication site can be designated as a home site in SharePoint.

The following is the high-level plan for shaping your home site:

- If your organization does not have a home site, plan it first by creating a new communication site or choosing an existing communication site to be a home site.

- From the SharePoint Admin Center, set the communication site as a home site for your organization.

- The home site should be accessible to everyone in your organization.

Setting up a home site requires everyone's involvement from stakeholders to employees. The following are a few points to consider for designing a better home site.

Stakeholder Engagement

Since the home site is a gateway to your organization's intranet, it is important to prioritize the content and resources that are relevant to employees. It is critical to get aligned with your business and stakeholders to decide the content to prioritize. Meet with stakeholders to plan what content to surface. Decide what content to highlight, where to place the content, etc.

Enable Engaging Employee Experience

The home site should be employee-centric. It is a place for everyone in the organization to stay up-to-date with the information. Global navigation should be planned for better user engagement. Define a consistent look and feel on the home site by applying the organization-specific theme, logo, etc.

Plan for Navigation

The important content should be available easily to everyone, instead of searching for it. Not all the content can be placed on the home site or is relevant on the home site but is still important. The navigation should enable everyone to browse important content in the organization. Plan for better navigation with hub sites or global navigation.

Personalize the Content

As you can have only one home site per tenant, use audience targeting on the content including news, global navigation links, and web parts to target the relevant content to the users.

Define Microsoft 365 groups or email-enabled security groups to target the content to a specific set of users. Consider using dynamic membership groups to be compliant with the organization's Joiner, Mover, and Leaver (JML) process.

Monitor the Performance

The SharePoint home site is one of the heavily trafficked sites in an organization. Always make sure the home page is healthy and performant.

Home Site Superpowers

When you designate a communication site as a home site in SharePoint, it gets some superpowers to make an engaging SharePoint landing experience.

Official Source of News

The home site is the official source of information for news and updates to the employees. News posts created from the home site are considered as official organizational news and always take precedence on the home site and SharePoint start page.

As shown in Figure 4-2, you can make out that news created from the home site is displayed as a priority on the SharePoint start page. The news also has a special visual appearance as a color block.

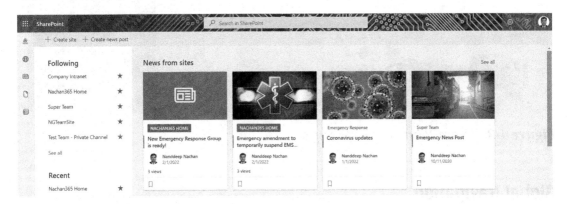

Figure 4-2. *SharePoint start page*

A communication site set as the home site automatically becomes an organization news site by default. We will explore more about setting up an organization news site in Chapter 7.

Home Site Features

With a home site set up, an organization can benefit from the following features.

Search Content Across an Intranet

From the home site, employees can search for content including news, sites, people, and files across the intranet.

Figure 4-3 shows the search user experience in the SharePoint home site.

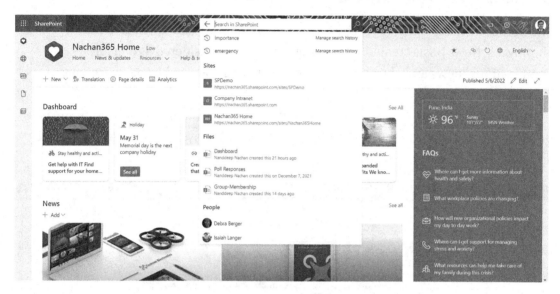

Figure 4-3. *SharePoint home site search*

Global Navigation

Global navigation helps to define useful links to employees that will be available to them throughout all the SharePoint sites they navigate. Organizations can benefit from this feature to highlight important resources to their employees.

SharePoint App Bar

The app bar is a sidebar available in the left navigation on all SharePoint sites. It features global navigation. It provides a personalized experience for the users by displaying My Sites, My News, My Files, and My Lists.

We will explore more about global navigation and the app bar in Chapter 5.

Build the Home Site

After adequate planning and agreement with all stakeholders on what content to surface and where to place it on the home site, it is now time to involve technical experts to create a site in SharePoint and turn that into a home site.

It is important to note the following points on why, what, and how before setting up a home site:

- The home site is a prerequisite for Viva Connections.

- The home site should be a modern communication site.

- It can be created via the SharePoint Admin Center or PowerShell.

- The SharePoint administrator or Global administrator can provision a home site.

- There can be only one home site per tenant, as of this writing.

- It generally takes 10 to 15 minutes for the home site to take effect.

Set Up a SharePoint Site

The first step is to create a SharePoint site for your employee engagement. The SharePoint tenant comes with a default site called a *root site*. There is a subtle difference between the root site and the home site. We will explore it a bit later.

Follow these steps to create a new SharePoint site:

1. Open the SharePoint Admin Center.

2. Under **Sites**, click **Active Sites**.

3. Click **Create**.

4. Choose a Communication site.

Figure 4-4 shows the site creation experience in the SharePoint Admin Center.

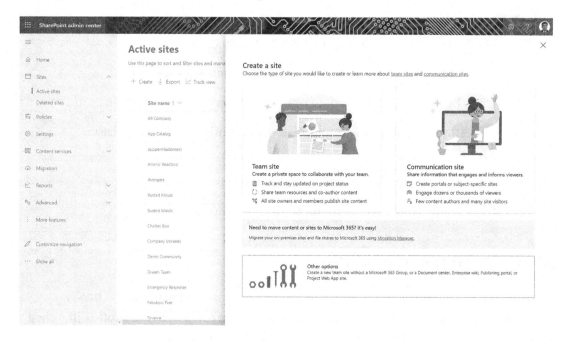

Figure 4-4. *Creating a SharePoint communication site*

Apply a Site Template

Once a site is provisioned, click Settings ➤ Apply a site template. You can choose
the Microsoft-provided templates as a starting point to design your site or you can
choose the one from your organization, which your developers have designed for your
organization using site scripts and site designs.

Figure 4-5 shows how to choose a template for the SharePoint site.

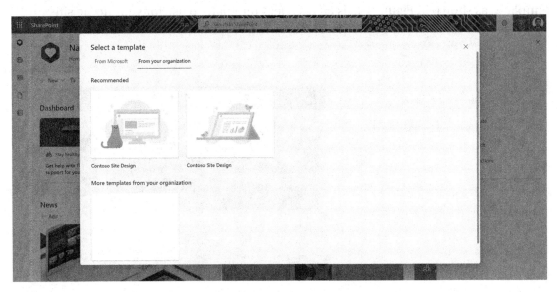

Figure 4-5. *Choosing a site template*

SharePoint Lookbook

A SharePoint lookbook (`https://lookbook.microsoft.com`) is a set of SharePoint templates provided by Microsoft that help you to quickly create nice-looking sites in minutes. You can simply choose and install a template in your SharePoint tenant to get started.

If you are unsure of where to start and which template to choose, then "The Landing template", as shown in Figure 4-6, is an excellent template to use for your home site.

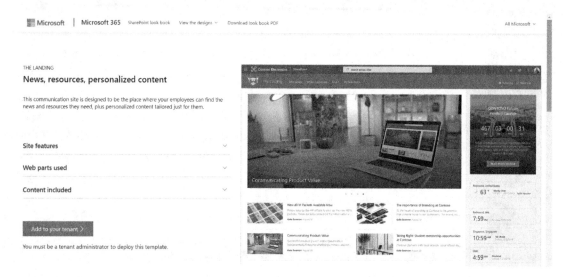

Figure 4-6. *The Landing template*

It is important to note that the SharePoint lookbook provides you with templates that are responsive and customized for a specific scenario. It includes the site features, web parts, and content, including sample modern pages, news articles, custom welcome page structure, images, and office documents.

Set the Site as the Home Site

Once you are ready with your SharePoint site, follow these steps to promote the site as a home site:

1. Open the SharePoint Admin Center.

2. From the left menu, click **Settings**.

3. Click **Home site**.

4. Specify the site URL.

5. Click **Save**.

Figure 4-7 shows how to set the home site in the SharePoint Admin Center.

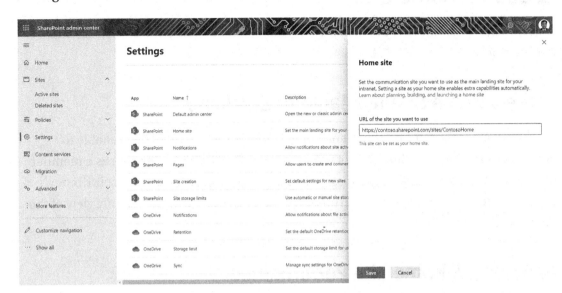

Figure 4-7. *Setting the home site in the SharePoint Admin Center*

PowerShell

If you are an administrator, you can follow the PowerShell approach as follows:

1. Download and install the latest version of **SharePoint Online Management Shell**.

2. Open PowerShell with administrator privileges and log in to SharePoint Online using the following cmdlet:

   ```
   Connect-SPOService -Url https://<domain>-admin.sharepoint.com
   ```

3. Set a home site using the following cmdlet:

   ```
   Set-SPOHomeSite -HomeSiteUrl <siteUrl>
   ```

Permissions

At a minimum, a SharePoint administrator role is needed to create a site and set it as a home site.

Launch a Home Site

After you build a home site, the next phase is to launch the home site and monitor its performance.

Make a Home Site Available to Everyone

The home site is the landing experience for all employees. It should be available to everyone in the organization. Do not forget to share the site with everyone as a member or a visitor. With the member permission level, employees will be able to contribute content, whereas with the visitor permission level they have only a read-only view of the home site.

Monitor the Home Site Performance

The home site is one of the high-traffic sites in your organization. Therefore, it should be optimized for performance. The pages should be high-performing and responsive so that the content can be delivered faster to employees. Specifically, the home page of the home site should be high performing, since the home site is a gateway to your intranet, and it should handle traffic coming from Viva Connections app inside Microsoft Teams.

Page Diagnostics for SharePoint Tool

The Page Diagnostics for SharePoint tool is helpful to analyze the performance of modern and classic SharePoint pages. It is available as a browser extension in the Microsoft Edge and Google Chrome browsers.

Follow these steps to install page diagnostics:

1. In the browser, find and install an extension named **Page Diagnostics for SharePoint**.

2. Run the extension on the home page of the home site to measure the performance.

Measure Site Performance

As shown in Figure 4-8, follow these steps to measure the performance of the home site:

1. Open the SharePoint home site.

2. From the **Settings** menu, click **Site performance**.

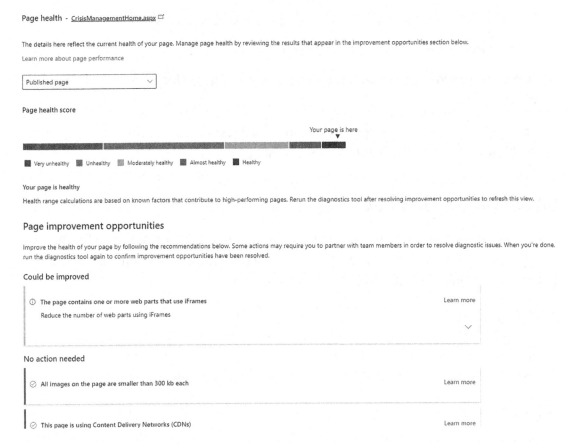

Figure 4-8. *Site performance*

The site performance page will display the page score in the range of Very unhealthy, Unhealthy, Moderately healthy, Almost healthy, and Healthy. The page will also suggest improvement opportunities.

It is important to work on the improvement opportunities and make your home page performant.

Enable Public CDN

It is recommended to enable a public CDN. The CDN hosts static assets such as images, style sheets, JavaScript files, etc. The CDN provides better performance on SharePoint pages by caching the static assets, which helps to reduce the latency.

CDN has two basic types:

- *Public CDN*: Used for serving static assets like JS and CSS files

- *Private CDN*: Used for serving images

Execute the following commands in the SharePoint Online Management Shell to enable the CDN:

```
Connect-SPOService -Url https://<Tenant>-admin.sharepoint.com
Set-SPOTenantCdnEnabled -CdnType Both -Enable $true
```

Schedule the Site Launch

The site launch scheduler helps organizations to carry out a phased rollout in batches to target the users by defining waves. The launch of each wave provides the flexibility to gather user feedback and improve the user experience.

Prerequisites

Before launching the site scheduler tool, make use of site permissions (owner, member, and visitors) to add users to the site based on the function they will perform.

Prepare

As shown in Figure 4-9, follow these steps to prepare a site for launch:

1. Open the SharePoint home site.

2. From the Settings menu, click Schedule site launch.

3. Review the site information.

4. Make sure your home page is healthy.

5. Click Next.

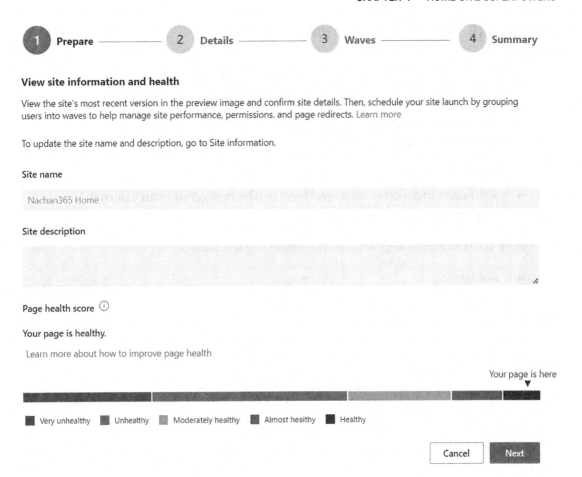

Figure 4-9. *Preparing site launch*

Details

Specify the number of expected users. The scheduler will define the number of waves based on this selection.

- *Less than 10,000 users*: Two waves

- *10,000 to 30,000 users*: Three waves

- *30,000 to 100,000 users*: Five waves

- *More than 100,000 users*: Five waves, but as mentioned creates a Microsoft support ticket to ensure the site's launch goes smoothly

Specify the Type of Redirection

- *Send users to or from an existing SharePoint site*: Users from the active wave will be redirected to the new modern SharePoint portal.

- *Send users to an autogenerated temporary page*: Users from the pending waves will be redirected to the autogenerated temporary page.

- *Send users to an external page*: Users will be navigated to an external URL until a wave is launched to users.

Figure 4-10 outlines the experience to define the site launch.

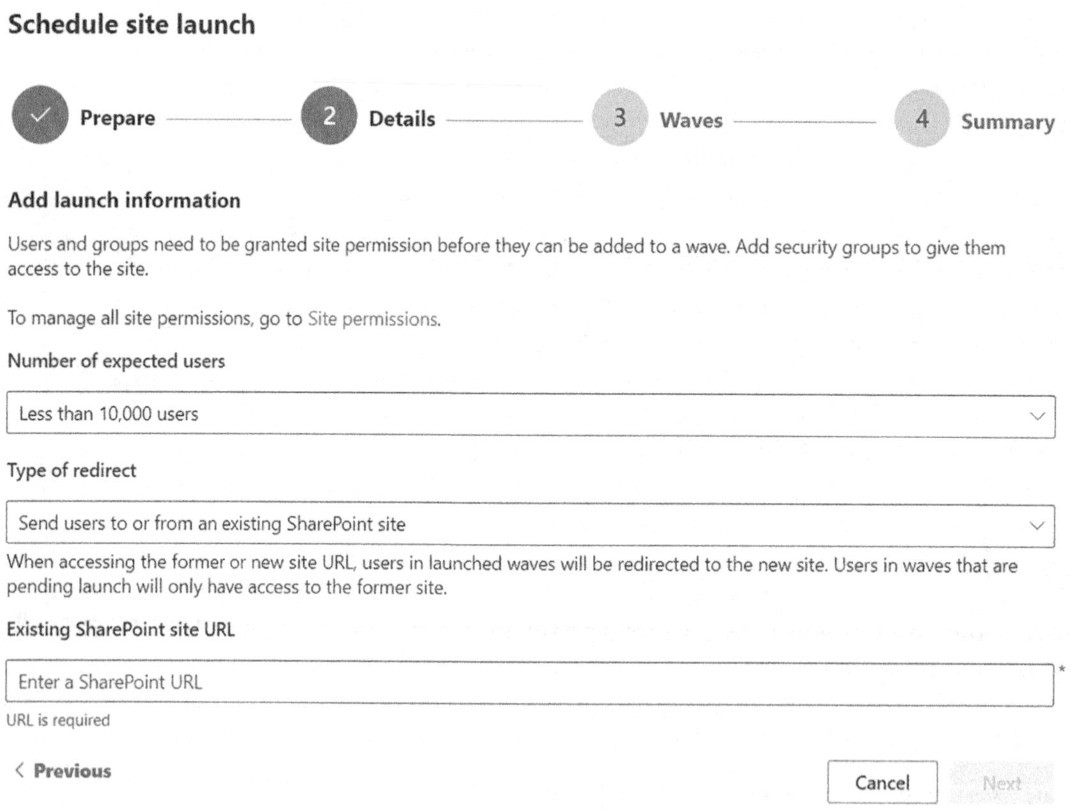

Schedule site launch

✓ **Prepare** ———— ② **Details** ———— ③ **Waves** ———— ④ **Summary**

Add launch information

Users and groups need to be granted site permission before they can be added to a wave. Add security groups to give them access to the site.

To manage all site permissions, go to Site permissions.

Number of expected users

Less than 10,000 users	⌄

Type of redirect

Send users to or from an existing SharePoint site	⌄

When accessing the former or new site URL, users in launched waves will be redirected to the new site. Users in waves that are pending launch will only have access to the former site.

Existing SharePoint site URL

Enter a SharePoint URL	*

URL is required

‹ **Previous**   Cancel   Next

Figure 4-10. *Defining site launch*

Waves

Based on your selection during preparation, you will see defined waves on this page. You can specify the schedule for each wave by adding 20 security groups per wave.

Figure 4-11 shows how to schedule the site launch.

Schedule site launch

Break your audience up into waves

Based on the expected number of users and to ensure a performant site, we recommend that you launch in 2 wave(s). Choose the date and time for each wave and add up to 20 groups per wave. Add and edit wave details up until the scheduled launch of each wave.

Waves will launch in the time zone for this site: (UTC+05:30) Chennai, Kolkata, Mumbai, New Delhi.

Users who have permission to view this site but are not included in a wave will get access after the last wave is launched.

Wave 1

| Tue, Feb 15, 2022 | | 9:00 AM | |

SM Sports Lovers Members ✕ Enter up to 19 security groups

Wave 2

| Tue, Feb 22, 2022 | | 9:00 AM | |

SA SPO Access ✕ Enter up to 19 security groups

Users exempt from waves ⓘ

NN Nanddeep Nachan ✕ Enter up to 49 users and security groups

‹ **Previous**   Cancel   **Next**

Figure 4-11. *Define waves*

Summary

As shown in Figure 4-12, review and confirm the launch details on this page.

Schedule site launch

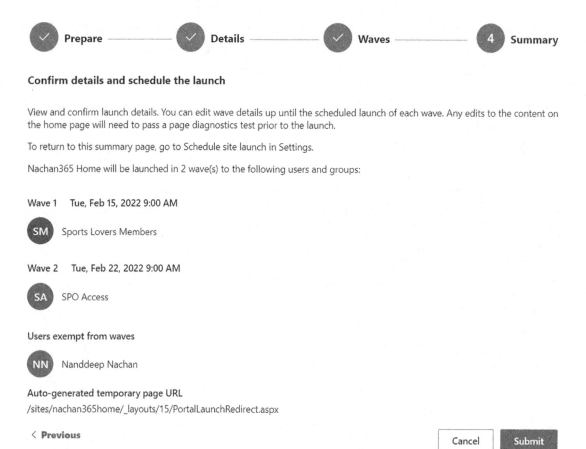

Confirm details and schedule the launch

View and confirm launch details. You can edit wave details up until the scheduled launch of each wave. Any edits to the content on the home page will need to pass a page diagnostics test prior to the launch.

To return to this summary page, go to Schedule site launch in Settings.

Nachan365 Home will be launched in 2 wave(s) to the following users and groups:

Wave 1   Tue, Feb 15, 2022 9:00 AM

SM   Sports Lovers Members

Wave 2   Tue, Feb 22, 2022 9:00 AM

SA   SPO Access

Users exempt from waves

NN   Nanddeep Nachan

Auto-generated temporary page URL
/sites/nachan365home/_layouts/15/PortalLaunchRedirect.aspx

‹ Previous   Cancel   Submit

Figure 4-12. *Site launch summary*

Track the Home Site Usage

After launching the home site, keep tracking the site usage to analyze the user engagement and take the necessary actions to increase the engagement. Usage data is aggregated and displayed based on the Coordinated Universal Time (UTC). The calculation algorithm of page views is designed to filter out repetitive, continual operations by the same user on the same item, such as when a user repeatedly refreshes the page.

As shown in Figure 4-13, follow these steps to track the site usage:

1. Open the SharePoint home site.

2. From the Settings menu, click Site contents.

3. Click Site usage.

4. The page will display the user engagement with the site.

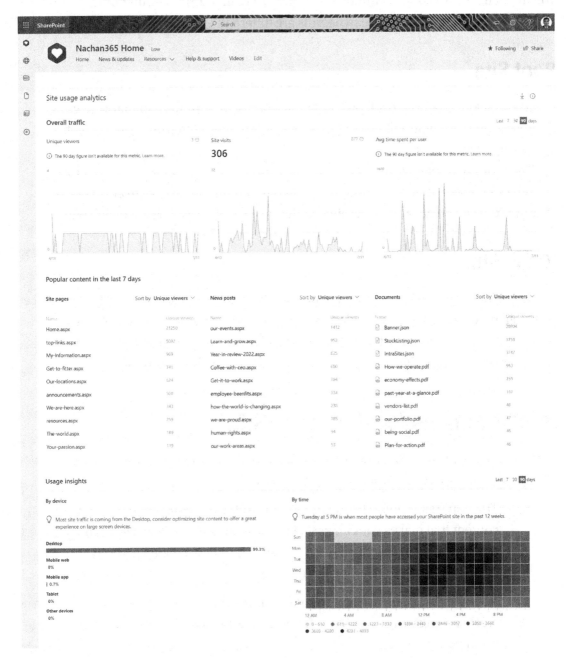

Figure 4-13. *Site usage analytics*

Home Site vs. Root Site

You might hear a lot about terminologies being used on the SharePoint home site and root site. Let's get into how these two terms are different.

Root Site

When you set up your Microsoft 365 tenant by specifying your domain name (e.g., Contoso), by default you will see a SharePoint site created at `contoso.sharepoint.com`. This site is your root site.

The root site is mandatory for each tenant, and it cannot be deleted. All Microsoft 365 tenants created after April 2019 have a modern communication site available as a root site. You can create additional sites under the `/sites` or `/teams` managed path.

Home Site

A SharePoint home site is a communication site that can be set as the landing experience of the SharePoint intranet. It provides an engaging experience for your employees by bringing together news, articles, and events relevant to them. As of today, you can designate only a single site as a home site. The root site can be a home site.

Best Practices for the Home Site

As the home site provides the landing experience of the SharePoint intranet, one should consider the following best practices to plan it better:

- The home site should be inclusive of all audiences. Surface the content that makes your users feel more connected. This will help an organization achieve the main purpose of building a digital gateway to your organizational information.

- It should be responsive and should be accessible on any device to create an engaging experience for both information workers and frontline workers.

- As the home site is a gateway to your intranet, expect huge traffic on it. Continuously monitor and optimize the performance of the home site.

- Plan your global navigation carefully, because it will showcase the links to important resources. This will help your users to navigate to content easily rather than searching for it.

- Track the home site usage to see the user engagement.

- Use all possible communication mediums (e.g., Yammer, Microsoft Teams, emailing the banners) to promote and spread the word about the home site.

- Make sure the home site is accessible to every employee of your organization.

- Try to have the root site as a home site to avoid any confusion among your users between the two.

- Since the news published from the home site always takes precedence on the SharePoint home site and start page, that news should be relevant to the organization.

- Set up the content approval flow to ensure verified and quality content will be published on the home site.

Conclusion

A home site is generally a SharePoint communication site that acts as the face of your organization's intranet. We have briefed you on the key concepts to plan, build, and launch a home site; understand the home site superpowers; and explore the SharePoint templates for the home site.

In the next chapter, you will learn about the importance of app bar and global navigation.

## CHAPTER 5

App Bar and Global Navigation

The app bar is designed to improve the navigation experience of users as well as dynamically display personalized content. The SharePoint app bar displays important organizational elements as well as personalized resources. It is simply a place to stay on top of your organization's resources as well as news and resources personalized for you.

In this chapter, you will learn about the importance of the app bar and global navigation. Also, we will explore their roles in Viva Connections.

Note If you don't have an app bar, users will miss the navigation panel in the desktop experience as well as navigation elements in the Resources section of the mobile experience.

App Bar

The SharePoint home site defines the landing experience for an organization's intranet. A home site is a must-have to enable the app bar and customize it further.

As shown in Figure 5-1, the app bar provides the user with a curated experience of global navigation to find organizational content and resources defined by the site owner or authors. It also provides a tailored experience of My Sites, My News, My Files, and My Lists based on what an individual follows in SharePoint as well as popular content. The app bar is available as a left bar across all sites in SharePoint.

© Nanddeep Sadanand Nachan and Smita Sadanand Nachan 2022
N. S. Nachan and S. S. Nachan, *Up and Running on Microsoft Viva Connections*,
https://doi.org/10.1007/978-1-4842-8606-7_5

Figure 5-1. *SharePoint app bar*

The app bar includes the following elements:

- Global navigation
- My Sites
- My News
- My Files
- My Lists

Global Navigation

Global navigation enables employees to navigate to important resources in SharePoint, defined by the business owners. Global navigation is a set of links that defines the navigation of users across SharePoint and other important organizational resources. These usually include links to news, policies, and events from the organization.

Figure 5-2 shows the global navigation experience of SharePoint.

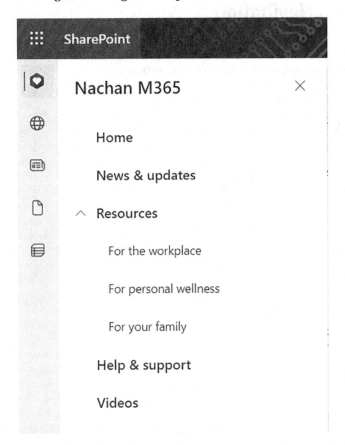

Figure 5-2. *Global navigation*

The home site is a primary prerequisite to set up global navigation. Without defining your home site, you cannot have global navigation.

Global navigation is the only customizable section in the app bar that can be defined by the administrator. The Viva Connections experience on both the desktop and mobile devices will display the global navigation to point users to the important resources. The global navigation is available in the Resources section of the mobile experience.

Prerequisites

The following are the prerequisites to enable global navigation:

- The home site set up in SharePoint

- Minimum site owner permission on the home site

Set Up Global Navigation

As shown in Figure 5-3, when you set a SharePoint site as a home site in the SharePoint Admin Center, it gets powered with two more options.

- Global navigation

- Set up Viva Connections

Figure 5-3. *SharePoint home site, Settings menu*

Follow these steps to set up global navigation:

1. Open the SharePoint home site.

2. From the Settings menu, click "Global navigation".

3. As shown in Figure 5-4, by default the global navigation is turned off. Turn it on by toggling the "Enable global navigation" menu.

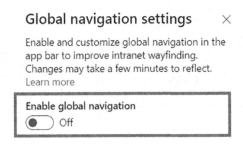

Figure 5-4. *Enabling SharePoint global navigation*

As shown in Figure 5-5, if the global navigation is turned off, the home menu in the app bar will navigate to the SharePoint start page.

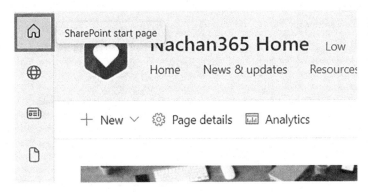

Figure 5-5. *App bar home pointing to start page*

Configure the Global Navigation

The configuration of global navigation includes the following elements.

Logo

Having a logo in the global navigation is optional. However, it is nice to have your organization's logo set as it will denote a familiar endpoint to the users. If you do not set a logo, the global navigation will continue to display the home icon for global navigation in the app bar.

The following are a few considerations for the logo:

- The logo should be 20×20 pixels.

- You should use the PNG file type.

- You should prefer a transparent background for the logo.

- Use the same logo in the Viva Connections app configuration for a consistent user experience in SharePoint and Microsoft Teams.

Title

The title field is mandatory, and it will be displayed at the top of the global navigation when opened from the app bar.

Figure 5-6 shows the placement of the logo and title on the global navigation.

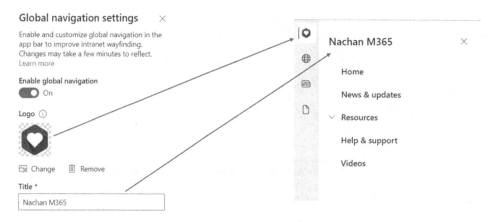

Figure 5-6. *App global navigation logo and title*

Navigation Source

The navigation source defines the links visible in the global navigation. Based on whether your home site is a hub site or not, you can select any of the following options:

- If a home site is not a hub site:

  - *Home site navigation*: Displays home site navigation

  - *Hub or global navigation*: Creates a secondary set of navigation

- If a home site is a hub site:

  - *Home site navigation*: Displays home site navigation

  - *Hub or global navigation*: Displays the home site's hub navigation

Figure 5-7 shows how to set up the navigation source of the global navigation.

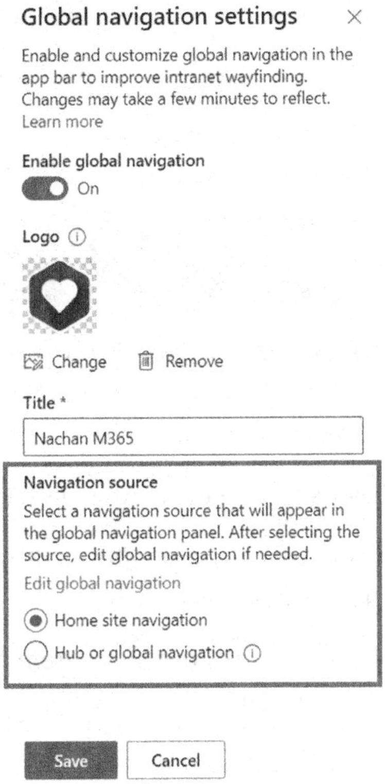

Figure 5-7. Global navigation, navigation source

Click "Edit global navigation" to update the global navigation.

As shown in Figure 5-8, in the global navigation, you can add menu items.

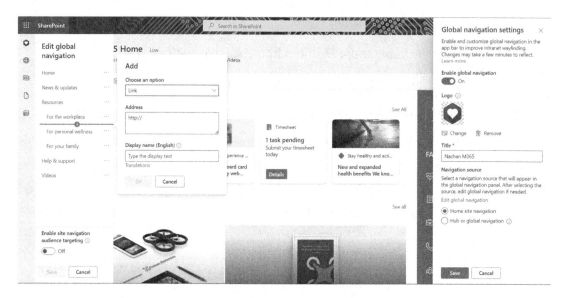

Figure 5-8. *Global navigation, adding menu items*

A menu item has the following properties:

- *Menu item option*: Choose to create a link or label.

- *Address*: This is available with the link option only. It defines the link to navigate to for a menu item.

- *Display name*: This is the name of the menu item that will be displayed on the global navigation.

- *Audiences to target*: If the "Enable site navigation audience targeting" option is turned on, you can specify the groups to target for a menu item.

Audience targeting will help to target the menu items to a specific set of people. You can specify a Microsoft 365 group, email-enabled security group, or dynamic group. However, you are limited to specifying only 10 audiences per menu item. If no audiences are specified, then everyone will have access to the menu item.

Global navigation is available only on modern SharePoint. If you are still using the classic SharePoint, then you will not be able to take advantage of the global navigation. Changes to the global navigation may take up to 24 hours to be reflected for users. Up to three levels of menu item nesting is supported in the global navigation.

Multilingual Support for Global Navigation

Global navigation supports specifying a localized text for each language your home site supports. With multilingual support, your employees can see the menu items from the global navigation in their preferred language.

Prerequisites

The following are the prerequisites to enable multilingual support for global navigation:

- The home site is set up to support multiple languages.

- The supported site languages are added.

As shown in Figure 5-9, when a SharePoint home site has multilingual support enabled, we can specify localized text for each supported language on the global navigation item.

Add

Choose an option

| Link | ⌄ |

Address

http://

Display name (English) ⓘ

Type the display text

Translations

OK   Cancel

Figure 5-9. *Global navigation, menu item translations*

After clicking the Translations link, we get an option to specify the localized text for each language that we have enabled support for. Figure 5-10 shows how to set the translations for the global navigation menu item.

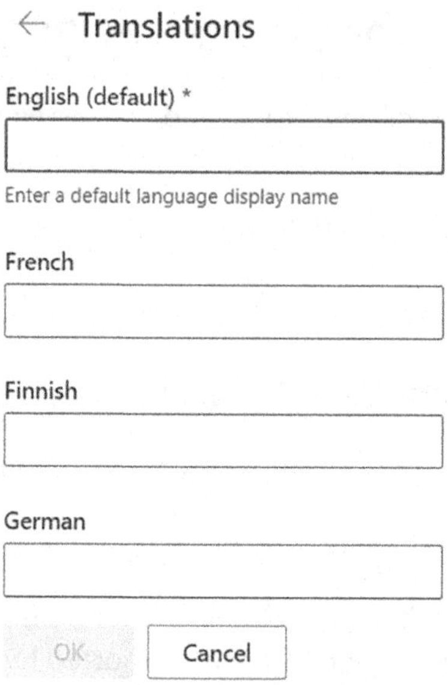

Figure 5-10. *Global navigation, menu item translations*

Governance for Global Navigation

Setting up global navigation is not a one-time activity. Although links in the global navigation do not change frequently, there should be governance set around this to ensure a fresh experience for users. Navigation should be consistent, organized, and guide users on what they need to find quickly.

The following is the governance checklist for maintaining the global navigation:

- Identify which links and labels should be on the global navigation.

- Identify the hierarchy of links on the global navigation.

- Identify who can see which links on the global navigation (audience targeting).

- Identify if the global navigation meets the needs of users.

- The global navigation should be planned with the end users in mind.

- The global navigation should reduce the amount of times users have to search for what they want to find.

My Sites

The My Sites feature is a tailored experience that displays the list of sites specific to the user based on the sites they follow or access frequently. A site can be followed by clicking a star while visiting a site. The followed site can be accessed from anywhere within SharePoint using the app bar menu.

Figure 5-11 shows the My Sites menu in the global navigation.

Figure 5-11. *App bar, My Sites*

My News

The My News feature is a tailored experience that displays the list of news specific to the user. The news recommendations are based on the communication sites users have access to. The priority is based on news from organizational news sites followed by sites accessed frequently by a user. The relevant news items displayed to the users are driven by insights from Microsoft Graph.

Figure 5-12 shows the My News menu in the global navigation.

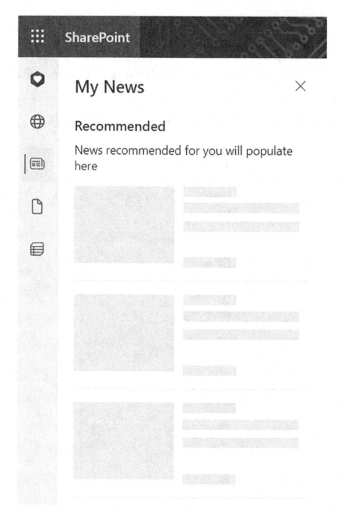

Figure 5-12. *App bar, My News*

My Files

The My Files feature is a tailored experience that displays the list of files that users are working on or accessing frequently from SharePoint and OneDrive. The relevant files displayed are driven by insights from Microsoft Graph.

Figure 5-13 shows the My Files menu in the global navigation.

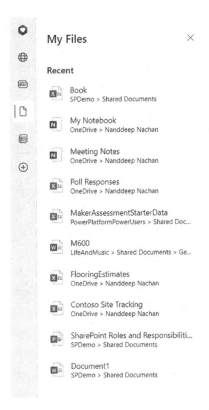

Figure 5-13. *App bar, My Files*

My Lists

The My Lists feature is a tailored experience that displays the Microsoft Lists specific to the user based on the lists they mark as favorite or access frequently. A list can be marked as a favorite by clicking a star while visiting the list. The relevant Microsoft Lists displayed are driven by insights from Microsoft Graph.

Figure 5-14 shows the My Lists menu in the global navigation.

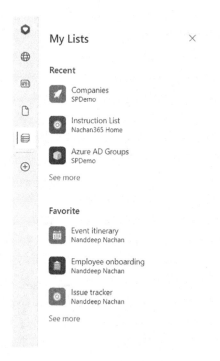

Figure 5-14. *App bar, My Lists*

Temporarily Disabling the SharePoint App Bar

The SharePoint app bar will be enabled by default for your organization. However, you can decide to delay the launch of the app bar to your users using PowerShell.

```
Set-SPOTemporarilyDisableAppBar $true
```

This setting can take up to an hour to take effect.

Please note that you cannot omit the app bar permanently; you can only delay its launch as per Microsoft's rollout plan.

Quick Tips for the App Bar

Make a note of the following points for the app bar experience:

- The app bar is available only on modern SharePoint.

- As the app bar is available on the left side, it might affect any page customization you have specifically with SPFx application customizer.

- Only global navigation can be configured from the SharePoint home page.

- Individual SharePoint app bar elements (i.e., My Sites, My News, My Files, and My Lists) cannot be disabled.

- Global navigation should be enabled for the resources to be displayed in Viva Connections.

- The user needs a minimum of read permission on the home site to view the global navigation links.

- When the global navigation is turned off, the home icon in the app bar will point to the SharePoint start page.

- The app bar is available on all modern SharePoint sites. It cannot be disabled on a specific site.

- Insights from Microsoft Graph play an important role in the user experience for My Sites, My News, My Files, and My Lists.

- Without Microsoft Graph enabled, the sites, news, and files experience will be degraded.

- The app bar will not be visible to external or guest users.

- The app bar can be disabled temporarily.

Role of the App Bar in Viva Connections

The Viva Connections app in Microsoft Teams will surface the SharePoint home site. The app bar will be visible by clicking the Viva Connections icon in the left rail of Microsoft Teams. The app bar will enable easy navigation and access to the global navigation, My Sites, My News, My Files, and My Lists inside Microsoft Teams to help users navigate and find content relevant to them.

Figure 5-15 shows the app bar experience of the Microsoft Viva Connections app in Microsoft Teams.

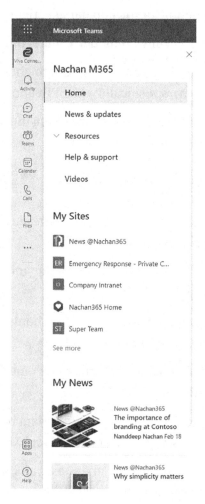

Figure 5-15. *App bar in Viva Connections app in Microsoft Teams*

Conclusion

The SharePoint app bar displays important organization elements as well as personalized content. The app bar is available as a left bar across all sites in SharePoint. The app bar provides the user with a curated experience of global navigation as well as a tailored experience of My Sites, My News, My Files, and My Lists.

In the next chapter, you will learn about the importance of the dashboard and how to add cards to the dashboard.

## CHAPTER 6

Authoring the Dashboard and Cards

The dashboard is at the center of Viva Connections. With Viva Connections, employees have access to all the important content and resources from various sources by reducing the context switching and getting all the updates in one place, that is, Microsoft Teams. Basically, a dashboard provides easy access to the information and presents another way to bring the content closer to your employees with the help of cards. The cards on the dashboard keep everyone up-to-date on the information and tasks they work on.

In this chapter, you will learn about the importance of dashboard and cards. Also, we will explore their role in Viva Connections.

Note Setting up the dashboard is not mandatory. However, it presents your employees with the cards to stay informed and offers easy access to the information.

Basics of the Dashboard

The dashboard acts as a digital toolset for your employees. The dashboard is an important element of the SharePoint home page and provides fast and easy access to information. In simple terminology, the dashboard is a way to present cards to the users. Each card represents a piece of curated information specific to the user and actions that they can take on the card. The dashboard cards can be targeted to users based on their role, department, or location to see the right tools for them to complete the tasks and

© Nanddeep Sadanand Nachan and Smita Sadanand Nachan 2022
N. S. Nachan and S. S. Nachan, *Up and Running on Microsoft Viva Connections*,
https://doi.org/10.1007/978-1-4842-8606-7_6

focus on important information. Therefore, a set of cards shown to frontline workers can be entirely different from the cards shown to information workers.

A dashboard helps employees to stay connected with organization resources such as seeing assigned tasks, sending and keeping track of approval requests, etc. At the same time, the dashboard allows you to offer partner integration with third-party vendors like ServiceNow, Workday, etc.

Dashboard Mobile Experience

As shown in Figure 6-1, the Viva Connections dashboard is available as a mobile experience on iOS and Android as part of the Teams app.

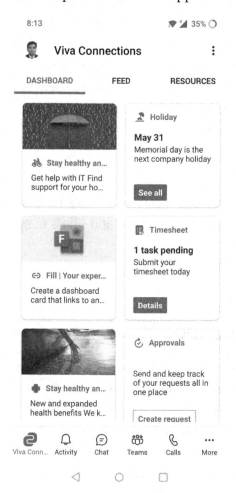

Figure 6-1. *SharePoint home site, Settings menu*

Dashboard Desktop Experience

For the desktop experience, a special web part called "Dashboard for Viva Connections" needs to be added to the home page of the SharePoint home site.

Figure 6-2 shows an example of the dashboard desktop experience.

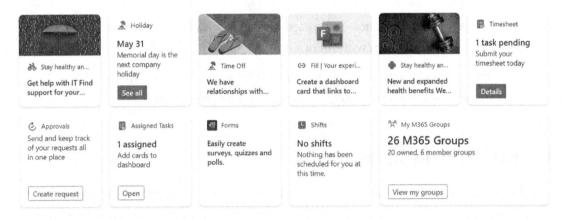

Figure 6-2. *Dashboard desktop experience*

Dashboard Exploration

The dashboard consists of medium and large cards. Generally, a large card is double the space of a medium card. While designing mobile and desktop experiences, it is essential to place the cards of various sizes together to create an enriching experience.

A user can interact with the card to perform the following actions:

- Open a SharePoint page.

- Navigate to external links.

- Access the Microsoft Teams app.

- Open a quick view as an action, which shows more information.

Let's go through the various elements that make up a dashboard.

- *Dashboard*: This is a place to show cards to users. It is available as the default tab on mobile devices. In a desktop experience, it is recommended to enable the dashboard on the home page of the SharePoint home site by configuring a web part called Dashboard for Viva Connections.

- *Layout*: The mobile experience supports a portrait layout. The desktop experience can show the Dashboard for Viva Connections web part based on the section layout.

- *Cards*: Cards are designed using an adaptive card, which is platform agnostic.

- *Quick view*: With a click of the card, the quick view provides more detailed information without opening an app.

- *Web view*: The web view can be opened from a quick view with a button click. It helps to load web pages or complex forms.

Define Your Dashboard

The dashboard is available as a feature of a SharePoint communication site. When a site is designated as a home site in SharePoint, we get an extra menu to configure Viva Connections from the Settings menu, as shown in Figure 6-3.

Figure 6-3. *Setting up the Viva Connections menu*

As shown in Figure 6-4, click "Set up Viva Connections" as a first step in creating the dashboard.

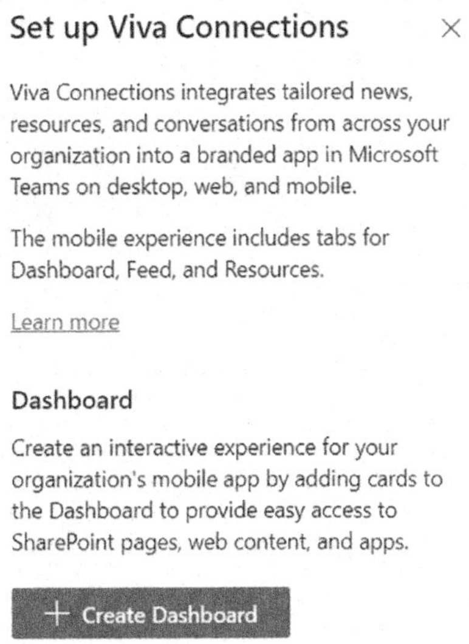

Set up Viva Connections   ×

Viva Connections integrates tailored news, resources, and conversations from across your organization into a branded app in Microsoft Teams on desktop, web, and mobile.

The mobile experience includes tabs for Dashboard, Feed, and Resources.

Learn more

Dashboard

Create an interactive experience for your organization's mobile app by adding cards to the Dashboard to provide easy access to SharePoint pages, web content, and apps.

+ Create Dashboard

Figure 6-4. *Creating a dashboard*

Clicking the "Create Dashboard" button will provision a special page named `Dashboard.aspx`, under the site pages library of SharePoint home site.

Once a dashboard page is created, the next time you click "Set up Viva Connections" in the Settings menu, you will see the "View Dashboard" button, which will take you to the `Dashboard.aspx` page.

Note   If you delete or rename the `Dashboard.aspx` page, you will be asked to create a dashboard again. Renaming any page to `Dashboard.aspx` does not make the page a dashboard page.

Multilingual Support for Dashboard

The Viva Connections dashboard now supports multiple languages. That means users will be able to view the dashboard in their preferred language.

Figure 6-5 shows the multilingual support for the dashboard.

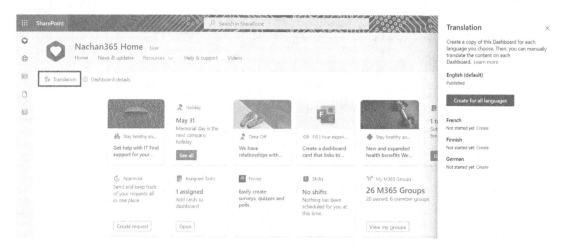

Figure 6-5. *Dashboard translation*

On the dashboard page, click Translation in the ribbon to enable a multilingual dashboard experience.

The language translators can translate the title, description, and cards to the requested language.

Add Cards to the Dashboard

By now we have our dashboard ready, so it is time to add some cards to it. The cards can be added for the Microsoft Teams app cards (e.g., Forms, Shift, etc.), web links (internal and external), third-party apps, and custom cards that you can build for your organization. Start by editing the Dashboard.aspx page. The page will let you place your cards for the mobile and desktop views.

Mobile View

The mobile view of the dashboard lets you place your cards for the mobile experience. As shown in Figure 6-6, you can place your cards on a screen by clicking "Add a card." It is important to note that the mobile view is just the view, not a separate dashboard.

Figure 6-6. *Mobile view for the dashboard*

Desktop View

As shown in Figure 6-7, switching to desktop view lets you design the experience for the desktop by adding cards of different sizes.

Figure 6-7. *Desktop view for the dashboard*

Add a Card

We can start by adding various built-in cards available by default. As shown in Figure 6-8, as you click "Add a card", you will notice a few cards you can add to the dashboard.

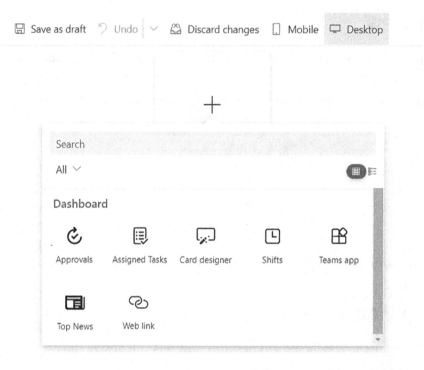

Figure 6-8. *Adding cards to the dashboard*

Let's explore the built-in cards one by one.

Web Link Card

A web link card helps you to navigate to internal (SharePoint site or page) or external links. As shown in Figure 6-9, configure the property pane to choose your options.

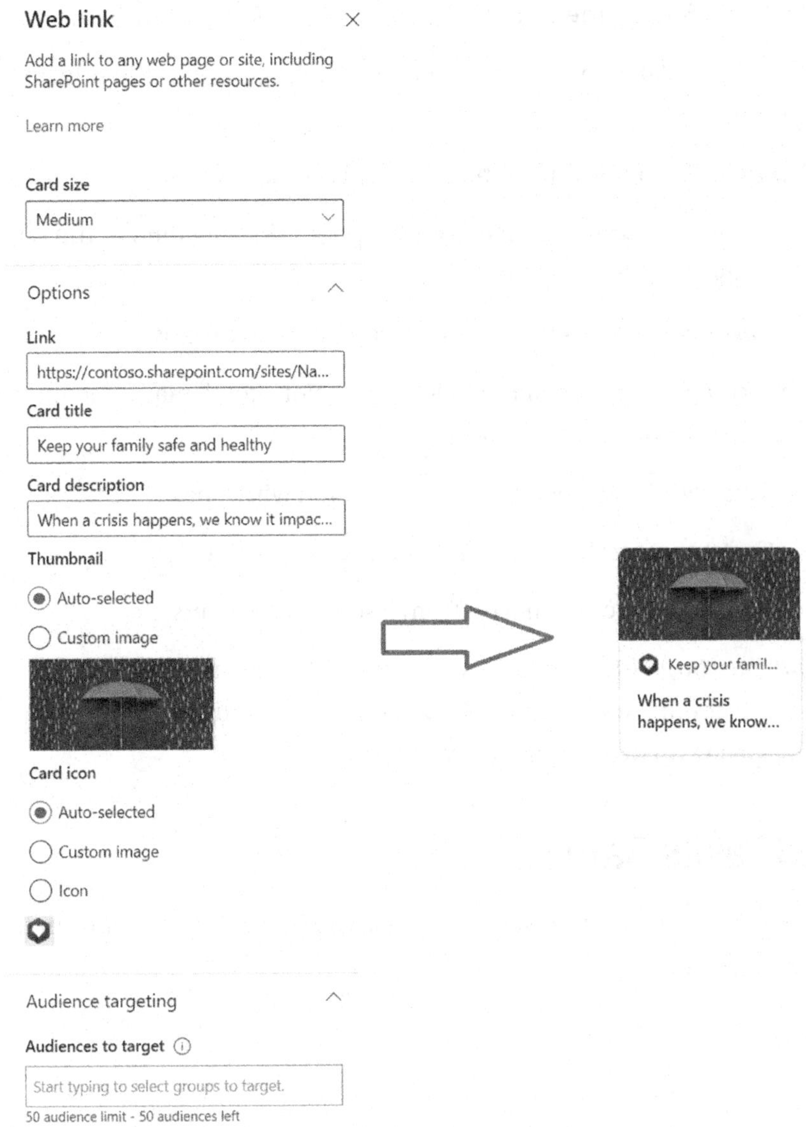

Figure 6-9. *Web link card property pane and preview*

Configure the properties as follows:

- *Card size*: Select Medium or Large, based on your layout preference.

- *Link*: Specify the URL to navigate to when clicking the card.

- *Card title*: Specify the text to be displayed on the top of the card.

- *Card description*: Specify the text to be displayed under the title on the card.

- *Thumbnail*: Specify one of the following options:

  - *Auto-selected*: The image from the page URL specified in the Link property will be displayed.

  - *Custom image*: A custom image can be set to display.

- *Card icon*: Specify one of the following options to display an icon on the left of the title on the card:

  - *Auto-selected*: Select the icon associated with a page.

  - *Custom image*: Select a custom image to display.

  - *Icon*: Select a custom icon from a set of stock icons.

- *Audience targeting*: Specify a Microsoft 365 group, mail-enabled security group, or dynamic group to target the card to display. You can specify up to 50 audiences to target.

Assigned Tasks Card

As shown in Figure 6-10, this card shows the tasks assigned to the user from the Tasks app in Microsoft Teams.

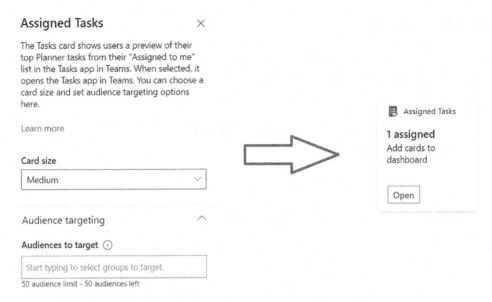

Figure 6-10. *Assigned Tasks card property pane and preview*

The card has a simple configuration of card size and audiences to target. As shown in Figure 6-11, when configured, clicking Open navigates to the Tasks by Planner and To Do app experience in Microsoft Teams.

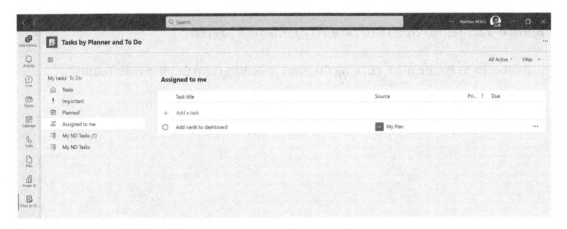

Figure 6-11. *Tasks by Planner and To Do app experience in Microsoft Teams*

Teams App Card

This card allows the creation of cards for Microsoft Teams apps. As shown in Figure 6-12, the card has a simple configuration of card size, Teams app to select, and audiences to target.

- "Select a Teams app" allows you to select an app from Microsoft Teams.

Figure 6-12. *Teams App card property pane and preview*

As shown in Figure 6-13, clicking the card opens the app in Microsoft Teams.

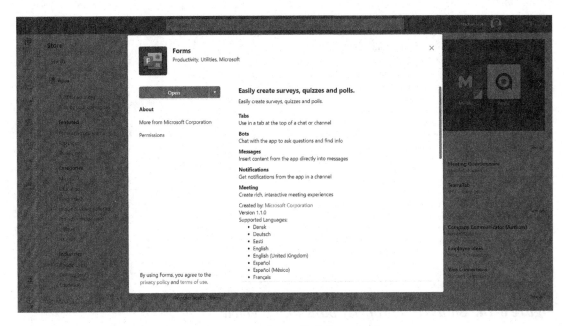

Figure 6-13. *Teams App experience when clicking card*

Shifts Card

This card allows tracking the shift information for the current or next shift from the Shifts app in Microsoft Teams. This also allows you to clock in and out and track break times.

As shown in Figure 6-14, the card has a simple configuration of card size and audiences to target.

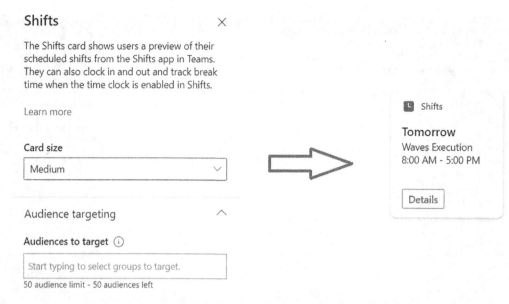

Figure 6-14. *Shifts card property pane and preview*

Approvals Card

This card allows you to send and keep track of requests from the Approvals app in Microsoft Teams.

As shown in Figure 6-15, the card has a simple configuration of card size and audiences to target.

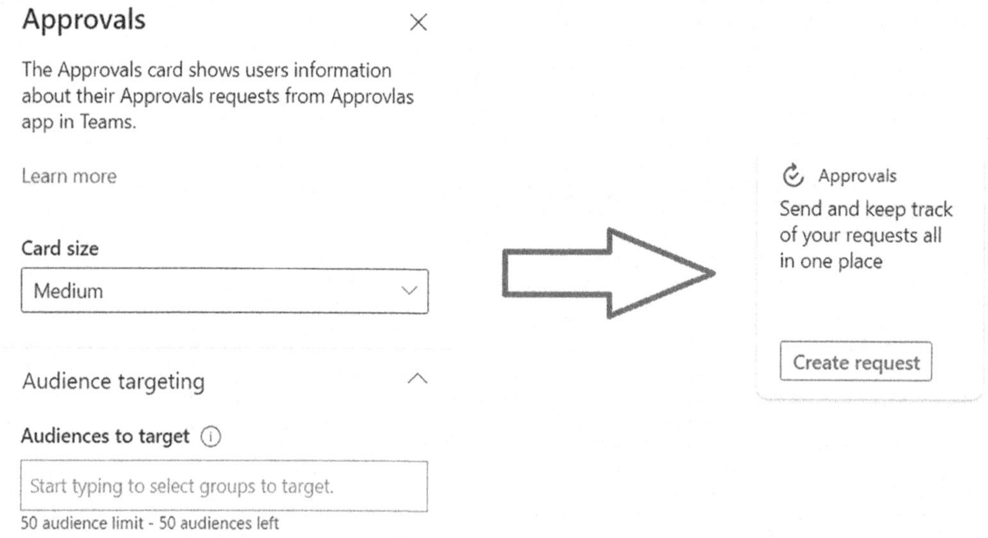

Figure 6-15. *Approvals card property pane and preview*

As shown in Figure 6-16, clicking the card opens the Approvals app in Microsoft Teams.

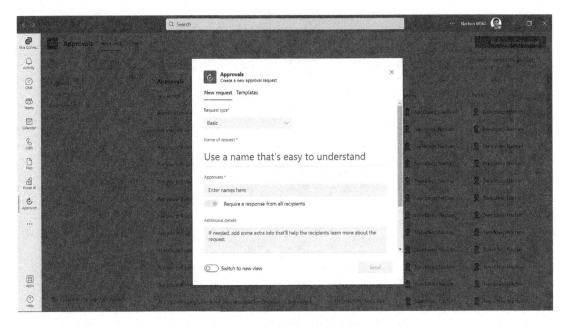

Figure 6-16. *Approvals app experience when clicking card*

Top News Card

The Top News link card displays the boosted news from SharePoint.

Card Designer Card

The "Card designer" card is a kind of low-code card that can be customized to some extent without custom development.

As shown in Figure 6-17, the card has various properties to configure under five sections.

Figure 6-17. *Card designer, with size and layout sections*

Section 1: Size and Layout

- *Template type*: The template for a card can be selected as one of the following:

    - *Heading*: Shows only the heading on a card

    - *Image*: Shows the heading and image on a card

    - *Description*: Shows the heading and description on a card

- *Card size*: Select Medium or Large based on layout.

Section 2: Card Content

As shown in Figure 6-18, this section defines the content of the card with the following properties.

Figure 6-18. *Card designer, "Card content" section*

- *Title*: Specify the title of your card.

- *Icon*: Specify a custom image or icon to be displayed alongside the title on the card.

- *Heading*: Specify the heading of the card that appears following the title.

- *Description*: Specify the description of the card that appears following the heading.

Section 3: Actions

As shown in Figure 6-19, this section helps to specify actions for clicking a card, as well as allows you to define buttons and their actions.

Figure 6-19. *Card designer, Actions section*

- *Card action*: Specify the action to take place with a click of a card. You can specify any of the following actions:

  - *Show the quick view*: You can specify the adaptive card–based quick view to show, which can be configured in the next section.

  - *Go to a link*: Specify a link to open when a card is clicked.

  - *Go to a Teams app*: Specify a deep link to the Microsoft Teams tab or channel.

- *Primary button*: This is an optional primary button to display on the card. You can specify a title and action on a button.

- *Secondary button*: This is an optional secondary button to display on the card. You can specify a title and action on a button. The secondary button is available only with the large card size.

Section 4: Quick View Layout and Data

As shown in Figure 6-20, this section helps you specify a quick view for a card that opens as another card when the viewed card is clicked. The quick view is created as an adaptive card.

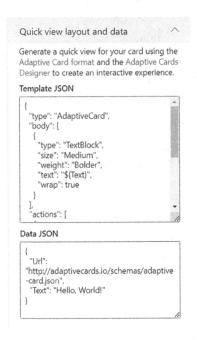

Figure 6-20. *Card designer, "Quick view layout and data" section*

- The section provides a sample template and data JSON as a base.

    - *Template JSON*: Defines the controls (e.g., TextBlock, button, etc.) on the quick view card.

    - *Data JSON*: Defines the placeholder data to be displayed in the template JSON. The placeholder in the template JSON is denoted in curly brackets, for example, ${Text}. The value will be replaced with these placeholders from the data JSON at runtime.

Section 5: Audience Targeting

Specify the M365 group, mail-enabled security group, or dynamic group to target the card to display. You can specify up to 50 audiences to target.

The card when configured displays as shown in Figure 6-21.

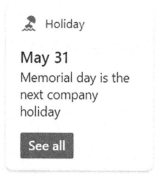

Figure 6-21. *Card designer preview*

When clicked a card, it displays the quick view, as shown in Figure 6-22.

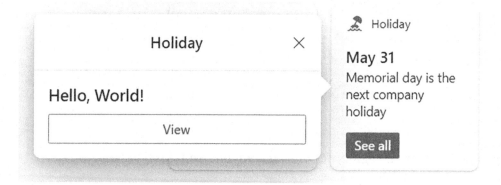

Figure 6-22. *Card designer, quick view*

Preview and Publish Dashboard

When you are done with adding and arranging your cards on a dashboard, it is always good to preview it to ensure the correct user experience before publishing it.

Figure 6-23 shows the preview and publish/republish experience of a dashboard.

Figure 6-23. *Previewing and publishing a dashboard*

The preview option enables you to preview of the user experience for each of the audiences applied on the dashboard, as shown in Figure 6-24.

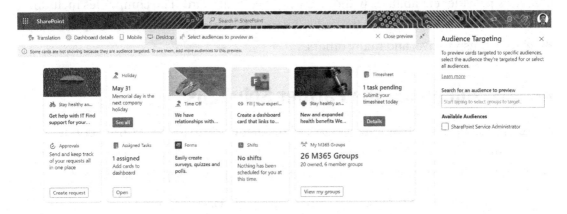

Figure 6-24. *Dashboard audience preview*

Partner Solutions

Viva Connections allows you to extend the dashboard by adding cards. Various partners and ISVs have already created experiences for IT, HR, finance, employee experiences, and other services that can be easily plugged into Viva Connections.

Microsoft has announced several partners for Microsoft Viva to deliver a seamless integration experience. Many partners have created cards for the Viva Connections dashboard. This integration enables using the power of partner solutions right within the dashboard.

- The partners are from various domains including the following:

  - *Workday*: Allows employees to access Workday insights and actions in the dashboard

  - *ServiceNow*: Brings the ServiceNow employee experience into the Connections dashboard (e.g., accessing the Employee Center, seeing all tasks assigned to them)

  - *Qualtrics*: Collects employee sentiment from their flow of work

  - *UKG*: Allows employees to access resources, request time off, and check pay statements without leaving the dashboard experience

Also, various other popular service providers are making their experience available to the Viva dashboard so that employees can perform their work and take advantage of service provider capabilities without leaving the dashboard. The companies include Moveworks, Limeade, Tribute, LifeWorks, Talentsoft, StandOut, EdCast, Zebra-Reflexis, BlueYonder, Espressive, and many others.

Access and Install the Partner Solutions

There is no single predefined process to add partner cards to the Viva Connections dashboard.

The following are the generic steps to add third-party cards to the dashboard:

1. IT admins can browse applications available via Microsoft AppSource (`https://appsource.microsoft.com`) or the SharePoint store.

2. Add the application to the App Catalog site in SharePoint.

3. Deploy the app.

4. Add the app to the dashboard.

It is advisable to work with the partner to make sure all the prerequisites are met and follow the process designed by them.

Custom Development

Every organization has various services and systems that are being used by their employees daily. With Viva implementation, organizations are looking forward to having all of the information in one place, i.e., in Microsoft Teams. Presenting employees with the information they need to work effectively can be achieved by developing custom cards on the dashboard.

If you are looking for an experience beyond what is offered by Microsoft's out-of-the-box cards, as well as the partner solutions, you can ask developers to build customized cards using the SharePoint Framework (SPFx).

SPFx version 1.13 and onward support creating engaging experiences with cards. We will cover more about that process in Chapter 11.

While planning for cards, follow this approach:

- Prefer to use the first-party cards available from Microsoft as your first choice.

- Alternatively, use Card designer cards as a low-code approach to building customized cards.

- Make use of cards available from partner solutions to take advantage of their capabilities without leaving the dashboard.

- Develop custom Adaptive Card Extensions (ACE) using the SharePoint Framework to build custom scenarios.

Employee Dashboard Example with Cards

With first-party, partner, and custom-built cards, organizations can build dashboards for employees by showcasing critical apps and useful resources. The dashboard will help employees to get important information and bring visibility to key metrics.

Figure 6-25 shows an example of an employee dashboard with cards.

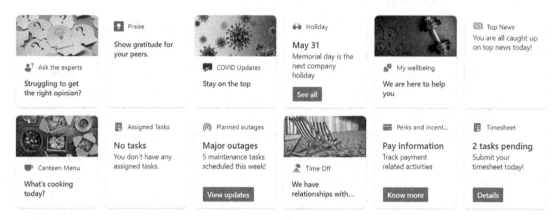

Figure 6-25. *Employee dashboard example with cards*

The cards should be inclusive for both frontline workers and information workers to surface the resources. The categories that can be covered by cards are as follows.

Employee Engagement

To foster user engagement and to help employees collaborate, the following cards can be placed on the dashboard:

- *Praise/Kudos*: Appreciate colleagues for their work.

- *FAQs*: List of common queries and solutions.

- *Discussions*: Forum for conversations.

- *Ask the experts*: Get help from experts by asking questions.

- *New Employee Onboarding (NEO)*: Guide new employees on tasks to perform.

- *My wellbeing*: Showcase how work-life balance is maintained for everyone with their engagement.

- *My Tasks*: Help employees to keep track of tasks they are working on.

- *Timesheet*: Help employees to submit timesheets.

Facilities

To make everyone aware of the facilities provided by the organization or in general, the following cards can be placed on the dashboard:

- *The canteen menu*: This makes it easy for employees to browse the food menu and place their order.

- *COVID update*: This helps organizations to keep their employees informed on the current COVID situation and guidelines.

- *Place a request*: This helps employees browse the facilities and place a request for one.

IT Support

To help employees and the IT support team track requests, the following cards can be placed on the dashboard:

- *Raise ticket*: This helps employees to raise a support ticket.

- *My tasks*: This helps IT to view and act upon the tasks assigned to them as an individual or group assignment.

- *Outage information*: This helps IT to communicate outages to employees.

Pay and Benefits

To make employees track their benefits and pay structure, the following cards can be placed on the dashboard:

- *Pay information*: This helps employees track their payment-related activities.

- *Perks and incentives*: This helps employees know their eligibility for any perks or incentives.

- *Vacation and leaves*: This helps employees track their vacation balance and apply for leaves.

Conclusion

The dashboard acts as a digital toolset for your employees. A dashboard helps employees to stay connected with organization resources. The dashboard consists of medium and large cards to create an enriching experience for employees. Microsoft has made available first-party cards to start creating simple yet powerful card experiences. Card designer is a low-code approach to extend it further. Custom Adaptive Card Extensions can be built using the SharePoint Framework. Various partners are rolling out their powerful experiences with cards.

In the next chapter, we will explore getting the content ready for the feed with SharePoint and Yammer.

CHAPTER 7

Define Your Content Feeds

With Viva Connections, employees can see the content relevant to them based on the resources they follow. The content is delivered to the users from various sources or feeds including SharePoint, Yammer, and Stream. The feeds provide a tailored experience to users by bringing the most relevant content to them. It is important to get your content ready for the content feeds using SharePoint, Yammer, and Stream.

In this chapter, you will look at the different ways in which organizations can publish content that appears in the Viva Connections feed and how organizations can get the most out of the feed by combining the different types of content.

Note To create an engaging experience for your employees with feeds, consider defining your content with both SharePoint and Yammer.

Basics of Feeds

Feeds provide a personalized view to your employees that shows news, conversations, and discussions relevant to them. A feed can surface the content relevant to the users from SharePoint, Yammer, and Stream. Users can see the content from the sites they follow or are a member of on SharePoint, as well as any community they follow on Yammer.

© Nanddeep Sadanand Nachan and Smita Sadanand Nachan 2022
N. S. Nachan and S. S. Nachan, *Up and Running on Microsoft Viva Connections*,
https://doi.org/10.1007/978-1-4842-8606-7_7

There are various factors behind how the feeds get delivered to the users, including the following:

- Which feed content is rolled up to the user?

- Which content takes precedence?

- How frequently does the feed get updated?

- How does the content get ranked?

- How can we shape the content in the feed?

User Experience for Feeds

Viva Connections provides a seamless user experience for both mobile and desktop users.

Mobile Experience

For mobile users, Feed is available as a tab in the Viva Connections experience, as shown in Figure 7-1.

Figure 7-1. *Viva Connections mobile experience, Feed tab*

Desktop Experience

On the desktop, the app bar shows the personalized feed using My Sites, My News, and My Files, as shown in Figure 7-2.

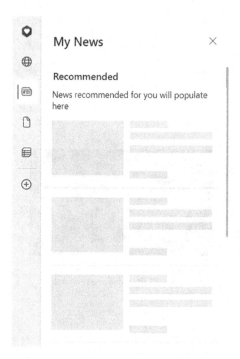

Figure 7-2. *Viva Connections, app bar*

As shown in Figure 7-3, SharePoint offers a useful web part named Feed for Viva Connections to show the content feeds.

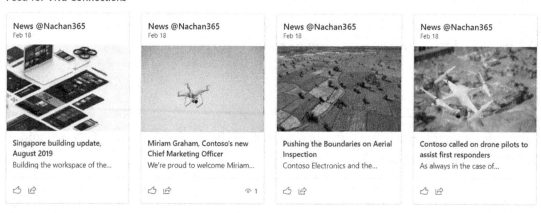

Figure 7-3. *Feed for Viva Connections*

Sources of Content Feeds

The content for the feeds is delivered from various sources across Microsoft 365 including the following:

- *News from SharePoint*: The news from the home site, organizational news sites, and sites you follow are shown.

- *Posts from Yammer communities*: Conversations from all company communities, communities you follow, and well-featured posts from public communities are shown.

- *Videos from Stream*: Stream videos published as video news links or embedded in the news posts are shown.

The content where the user has access (direct or as a group member) will be shown to the user, as shown in Figure 7-4.

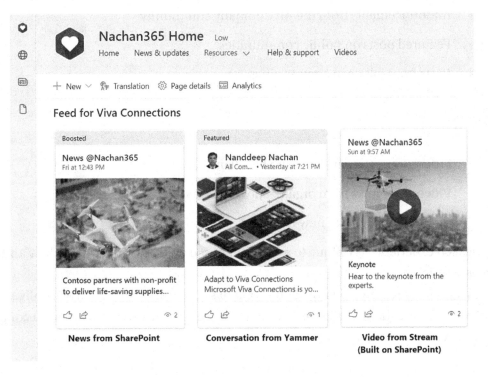

Figure 7-4. *Content feed from various sources*

In Figure 7-4, you can notice the content coming from various feeds including the following.

SharePoint

- News posts from the home site

- News posts from organizational news sites

- News posts from frequently visited and followed sites

- Boosted news from followed SharePoint sites

Yammer

- Posts from the All Company community

- Announcements from the All Company community

- Featured posts on public communities

- Posts from followed communities

Stream

- Videos from Stream (built on SharePoint)

- Video news links from organizational news sites

- Videos embedded in news feeds

The feed experience is unique to every user based on the content they follow and have permission to.

It is important to note that not all the content sources are required to be configured, but it's nice to have them configured to get the best engaging experience. Not all content sources have equal weight.

User Experience for a Content Refresh

From the users' point of view, it is important to understand how the content is delivered and refreshed for them.

When a home site is set up in SharePoint, it may take up to a week for content to appear in the feed. After this period, it may take up to an hour to get the latest content delivered to the feed.

For mobile users, they see the refreshed content every time they open the Viva Connections app or when they manually refresh with the pull-down action.

For desktop users, the content gets refreshed every time they visit the app or when they refresh manually by clicking the refresh link from a ribbon.

Content Ranking

To have an engaging user experience, it is important to present them with fresh content. If they see the same content each time they visit the Viva Connections, they might get bored and start to lose interest.

It is important to understand how the content is ranked and presented to the users.

Chronology

The content follows the chronological approach by sorting it into three buckets by its age.

- *0 to 4 days*: Fresh content, appears at the top

- *5 to 8 days*: A bit of old content, starts to push down in the feed

- *9 to 30 days*: Older content, pushed down in the feed

The fresh content always appears at the top. Figure 7-5 shows example content appearing in chronological order of age.

Figure 7-5. *Content chronology by age*

Content Promotion

Sometimes the chronology is not sufficient to present the fresh content to the users. The content creator has some control over the freshness of content by using features such as boosting news in SharePoint and featuring conversations in Yammer. The boosted and featured content is placed at the top of each bucket.

Based on the permissions, an individual will have access to part of each bucket. The content creators should ensure engaging content at each bucket.

User Actions on Feed

The success of Viva Connections depends on user engagement. Users can perform the following actions on the feed:

- Reactions to a post

- Comment on a post

- Reply to conversation

- Share the post

- Save post for later

Role of Content Creator

The content creator plays a limited but important role in presenting fresh content to the user. The content creator does not have huge control over the content to be seen by an individual. However, they can balance the needs of the business against the wishes of the audience.

The content creators can influence the content ranking in the following ways:

- *Promote important news*: Content creators can increase the visibility of official communications by using the boost feature on SharePoint.

- *Highlight important conversations*: Content creators can feature the conversations from Yammer public communities to bring visibility.

- *Publish from official sources*: Content creators can post the important content from the SharePoint home site or an organizational news site to be seen as important content, instead of posting it from any team or communication site. The content published from the official sources affects the ranking.

Feeds from SharePoint

Let's explore SharePoint as a source for feeds. Modern SharePoint news is a good candidate for the feeds. If a communication site is set as a home site, it is automatically configured as an organizational news site.

Organizational News Site

In a SharePoint intranet, we can designate a specific site as an organization-level news site. This site will act as an official source of information for the organization.

As shown in the Figure 7-6, the news from the organization's news site will always get a special appearance on the SharePoint start page.

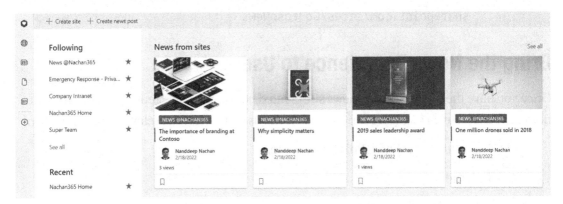

Figure 7-6. *News from the organizational news site on the SharePoint start page*

Designate a SharePoint Site as an Organizational News Site

Unfortunately, we do not have a UI option to designate a site as an organizational news site. You will need to use PowerShell for this purpose.

If you do not have a news site set up for your intranet yet, then you may consider using any of the lookbook templates from `https://lookbook.microsoft.com/` to start. Figure 7-7 shows an example of lookbook templates available for news.

SharePoint administrators can specify up to 250 sites as organization news sites. It is worth setting the home site as an authoritative organization news site as well. A communication site set as a home site automatically becomes an organization news site by default.

Follow these steps to set a site as an organizational news site:

1. Download and install the latest version of the SharePoint Online Management Shell.

2. Connect to SharePoint Online as a SharePoint administrator or Global administrator.

   - `Connect-SPOService -Url https://contoso-admin.sharepoint.com`

3. Set a site as an organizational news site by running the following command:

   - `Set-SPOOrgNewsSite -OrgNewsSiteUrl https://contoso.sharepoint.com/sites/ContosoNews`

Bring the News Experience to Users

Once you have the organizational news site created, follow the next steps on the SharePoint home site to create an engaging experience for the users to show the relevant news for them:

1. Navigate to the SharePoint home site.

2. Edit the home page.

3. Add the News web part.

Figure 7-7 shows how to add a News web part to the SharePoint page.

Figure 7-7. *Adding the news web part to home page*

4. Edit the web part to open the web part properties pane, as shown in Figure 7-8.

5. As shown in Figure 7-8, select "Recommended for current user."

Figure 7-8. *News web part, setting the news source*

6. As shown in Figure 7-9, optionally select and order news from the web part property pane.

Figure 7-9. *News web part, reordering the news*

7. The News web part will show the recommended news, as shown in Figure 7-10.

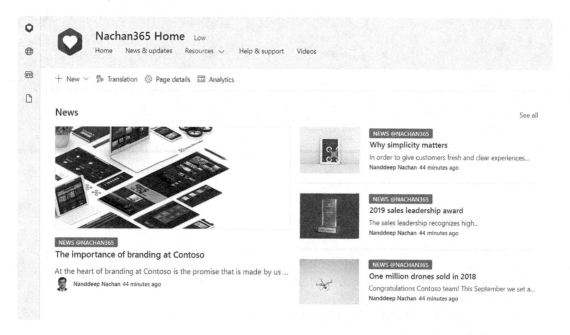

Figure 7-10. *News web part in action*

News Boost Feature

The boost feature in SharePoint prioritizes the news and announcements to make them visually appear at the top. The boosted news appears at the top in the Feed web part for Viva Connections and Viva Connection feeds.

Follow these steps to boost specific news:

1. Open a SharePoint news to boost.

2. In the Ribbon, click Boost.

3. In the panel, set the Boost option to On.

4. The news can be set to be boosted until a date.

5. If you choose to boost multiple news, order the news boost sequence.

Figure 7-11 highlights the steps to boost a specific piece of news in SharePoint.

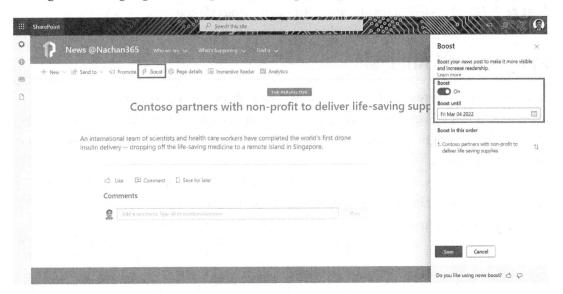

Figure 7-11. *News boost feature*

As shown in Figure 7-12, the boosted news will take visual precedence and will be denoted by the word *Boosted* on top of it.

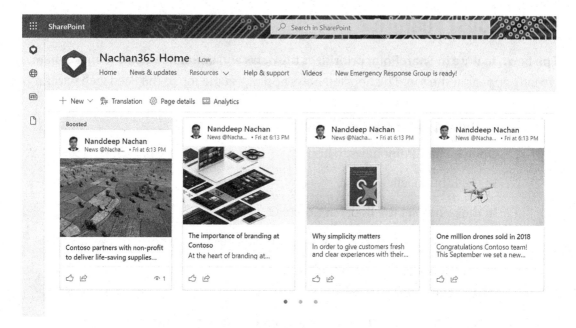

Figure 7-12. *Boosted news shown with visual precedence*

Insights and Analysis

To maintain the interest of end users in Viva Connections, it is important to carry out insights and analysis on the content presented to them. SharePoint Online provides out-of-the-box insights and analysis. It helps to understand the user engagement by their visits to the content.

Site and page-level analytics is by default enabled in SharePoint Online. The page owner or member of the site can view the analytics from the top of the page.

Figure 7-13 outlines the option to carry out page-level analytics.

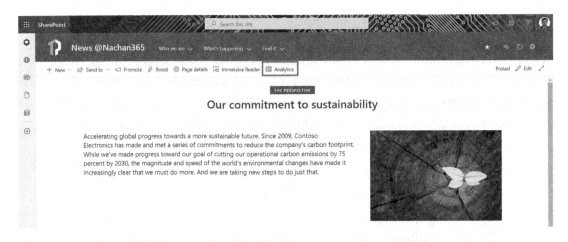

Figure 7-13. *SharePoint page analytics*

Usage data is collected and visualized based on Coordinated Universal Time (UTC). The daily unique viewers, views, average time spent per user, page traffic by time trends on the site and page can be viewed for the last 7, 30, and 90 days. The calculation algorithm of page views is designed to filter out repetitive, continual operations by the same user on the same item, such as when a user repeatedly refreshes the page.

Figure 7-14 shows the result of carrying out page-level analytics.

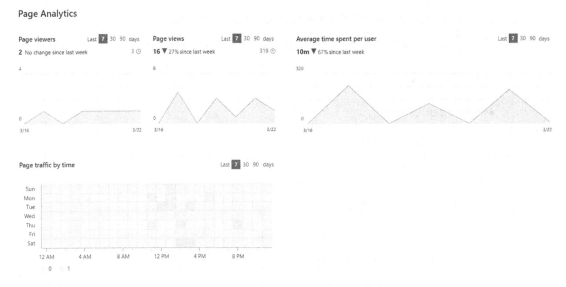

Figure 7-14. *SharePoint page analytics*

Yammer

In simple terms, Yammer is your organization's Facebook where everyone can share information, have meaningful discussions, reply, and add reactions to the discussions. It is your social network to engage with everyone in the organization. Connecting people through communities is at the heart of Yammer. Yammer helps to find like-minded people to give employees a connected feeling within an organization.

As an active user of Yammer, one should follow these tips to engage with colleagues:

- *Join a Yammer community*: A community in Yammer is formed by like-minded people to share ideas and carry out discussions. Join the communities of interest. Yammer will also suggest to you the communities to join based on your interactions on Yammer.

- *Create a Yammer community*: To connect like-minded, create a community if one does not exist. Invite your colleagues to join it.

- *Take a part in conversations*: Be part of the community by sharing your ideas and thoughts. Use Yammer's features to like and reply to the conversations. Grab the attention of colleagues by using the @mention feature.

- *Start a discussion in style*: While you start a discussion, choose whether it is a general discussion, a question, a poll, or praise for someone. Create an engaging message in Yammer in the following ways:

  - Ask a question

  - Poll the community

  - Praise a colleague

  - Share photos or video

  - Attach files

  - Link to internal or external resources

  - Express yourself with a GIF

  - Add a hashtag or topic

Feature a Conversation

You can amplify a Yammer conversation by using the Feature Conversation option in Yammer.

Follow these steps to feature a conversation in Yammer:

1. As shown in Figure 7-15, in a Yammer conversation, click the more options icon and select Feature Conversation.

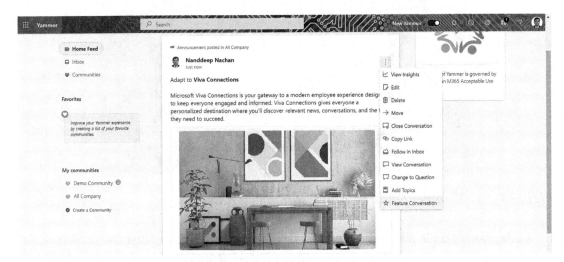

Figure 7-15. *Yammer feature conversation*

2. As shown in Figure 7-16, select the end date and time for the featured conversation.

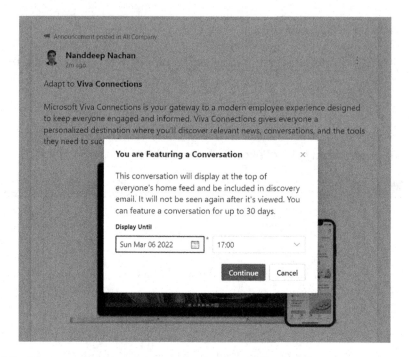

Figure 7-16. Yammer featured conversation end date

In the case of multiple featured conversations, the one expiring first will be shown at the top of the feed. There is no limit on the number of featured conversations that can be set. The admin's local time is considered for the feature end date and time. Conversations can be featured from both public as well private communities. It will be shown only to those who belong to those communities.

Deploy the Communities App

If the organization is already using Yammer, then this optional step is easy to configure to bring Yammer communities into Microsoft Teams. The Communities app is available in Microsoft Teams to drive engagement in organizations with Yammer communities. The app is enabled by default. Once configured, it works across web, mobile, and desktop experiences.

The Microsoft Teams administrator can pin the communities for everyone to collaborate better. Enabling the Communities app inside Microsoft Teams enables everyone to have a conversation with Yammer communities without leaving the Microsoft Teams experience.

Figure 7-17 shows the Communities app experience in Microsoft Teams.

Figure 7-17. *Communities app in Microsoft Teams*

Insights and Analysis

Insights are helpful to track user engagement. Insights in Yammer are available out of
the box.

Follow these steps to view the insights:

1. Head over to Yammer.

2. Open the Yammer community.

3. Click the About section.

Figure 7-18 shows an example of insights about the Yammer community.

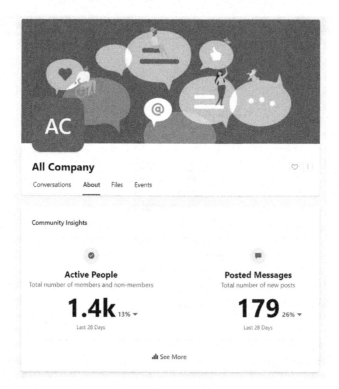

Figure 7-18. *Yammer community About section*

All insights are calculated in the Coordinated Universal Time (UTC) time zone. Community insights are available for periods of the last 7 and 28 days. A time interval can be selected from the drop-down list at the top. Also, community insights can be exported in CSV for time periods of the last 7, 28, and 365 days.

Click See More to view detailed insights about the Yammer community. It shows insights into people and content.

Active People

This section provides the number of active people in the community and their activity trends compared to the previous period. The user activities refer to posting, reading, and reacting to a message in the community.

These trends will help you to understand the user engagement in the Yammer community.

Figure 7-19 shows an example of Yammer insights on active people.

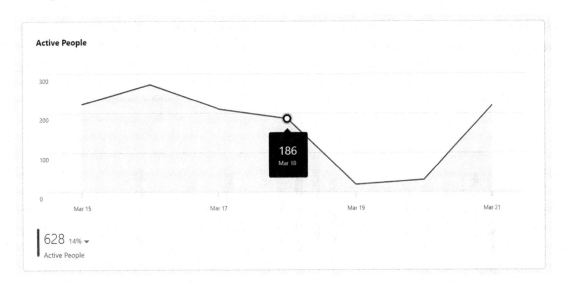

Figure 7-19. *Yammer insights on active people*

Active Members and Nonmembers

This section shows the activity of community members. Nonmembers are people who interact with the community but are not members of the community. As shown in Figure 7-20, the user activities include posting, reading, and reacting to a message in the community.

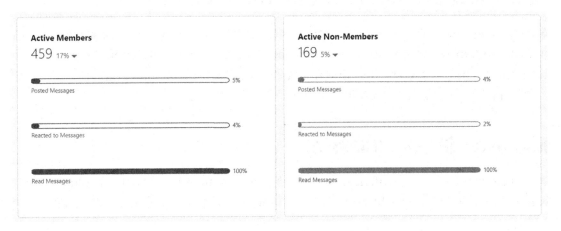

Figure 7-20. *Yammer insights on active members and nonmembers*

Content Insights

As shown in Figure 7-21, this section provides insights on messages posted, read, and reacted to in the community.

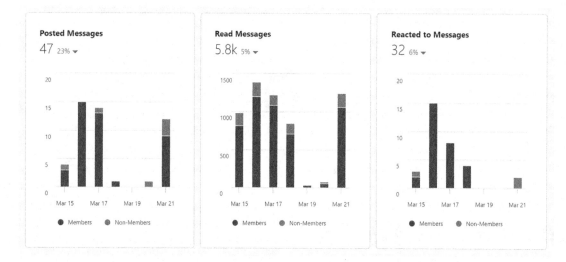

Figure 7-21. *Yammer insights on the content*

For public communities, any member of the Yammer network can see the insights. For private communities, only members of the community can see the insights.

Microsoft Stream (Built on SharePoint)

Microsoft Stream is a popular video app in Microsoft 365 suite. It helps users to create, manage, and discover the videos. The new version of Microsoft Stream has been revamped to be powered by the content management feature of SharePoint.

Steam has two versions, as follows:

Microsoft Stream (Classic)

The old version of Stream will now be called Microsoft Stream (Classic). The old version was an independent app, where videos were stored separately from other Microsoft 365 apps.

Microsoft Stream (Built on SharePoint)

The new version is referred to as Microsoft Stream (built on SharePoint). When you upload a video in the new version of Microsoft Stream, it will be automatically stored in SharePoint. The videos across all Microsoft 365 apps (SharePoint, OneDrive, Yammer, and Microsoft Teams) are referred to as Stream videos.

Migrating to Microsoft Stream (Built on SharePoint)

At the tenant level, you do not have to make any updates to migrate from the classic version to the new one. Microsoft will roll out the updates in phases.

The following are the points to consider for migration:

- You can migrate existing content from Stream (Classic) to Stream (built on SharePoint) at your own pace.

- The migration tool will be available in the SharePoint Admin Center from Microsoft for the content migration.

- Permissions will be migrated by the migration tool.

Video News Links

Videos are an engaging way to interact with the users. Videos hosted in SharePoint and OneDrive can be published to the Viva Connections feed.

Publishing video news links is a two-step process.

Step 1: Create a Sharing Link

Follow these steps to create a sharing link:

1. Select a video from SharePoint or OneDrive.

2. Click Share.

3. Specify the intended audience.

4. Copy a link.

Figure 7-22 shows an example of creating a sharable link to a video in SharePoint.

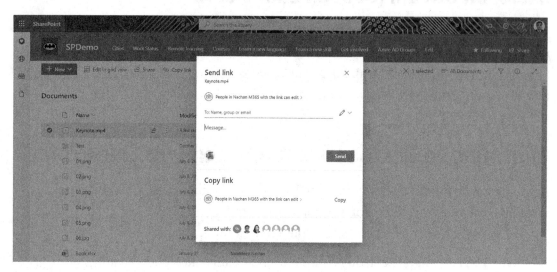

Figure 7-22. *Creating a sharing link for a video*

Step 2: Publish the Video as a News Item

Follow these steps to publish the video as a news item:

1. Navigate to a SharePoint organizational news site.

2. On the home page, click New ➤ Video news link.

Figure 7-23 shows an option to publish a video in SharePoint as a news item.

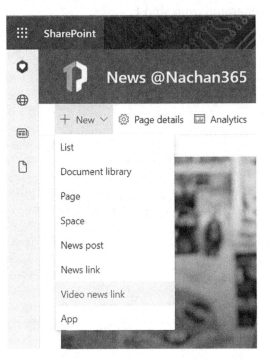

Figure 7-23. *Publish video as a news item*

3. As shown in Figure 7-24, in the configuration panel, specify the sharing link generated from step 1.

Figure 7-24. *Video news link properties*

4. Configure the properties for the video news item.

5. You may optionally specify a schedule to publish the video news item later. Also, you may specify audience targeting.

Videos from the following location are not supported in the Viva Connections feed:

- Videos from Stream (Classic)

- External videos (e.g., YouTube, Vimeo, etc.)

Conclusion

The feeds provide a tailored experience to users by bringing the most relevant content to them. A feed can generally surface the content relevant to the user from SharePoint, Yammer, and Stream. We explored getting the content ready for the content feeds using SharePoint, Yammer, and Stream.

In the next chapter, we will explore preparing a strategy to enable Viva Connections and its rollout in MS Teams.

## CHAPTER 8

Enable Viva Connections in Microsoft Teams

We now have our modern SharePoint intranet set up with home site superpowers, an app bar, and global navigation. We have our dashboard ready with cards to surface important resources in the Viva Connections app. We also have our feeds ready from SharePoint, Yammer, and Stream to organize the content better for our employees. It is time to enable the Viva Connections app in Microsoft Teams and roll it out to users.

In this chapter, you will learn about the process to configure the Viva Connections app in Microsoft Teams and define a rollout strategy.

Note   Viva Connections is an app inside Microsoft Teams that surfaces the SharePoint home site.

Understanding the Process

With everything set up nicely in the SharePoint intranet, it is time to get into Microsoft Teams and make the Viva Connections experience available to our users. Viva Connections is an app available inside Microsoft Teams.

As shown in Figure 8-1, it is a three-step process to roll out the Viva Connections experience to our users.

© Nanddeep Sadanand Nachan and Smita Sadanand Nachan 2022
N. S. Nachan and S. S. Nachan, *Up and Running on Microsoft Viva Connections*,
https://doi.org/10.1007/978-1-4842-8606-7_8

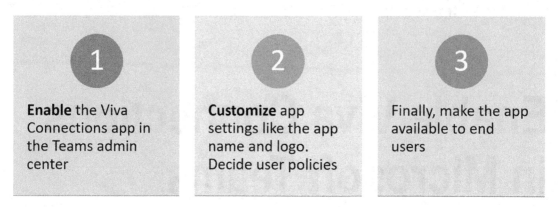

Figure 8-1. *Three steps process to roll out Viva Connections*

Permissions

The Microsoft Teams administrator or someone with a higher role can enable the Viva Connections app in Microsoft Teams from the Teams Admin Center (TAC).

Enable the Viva Connections App in the Teams Admin Center

There are two ways to enable the Viva Connections app.

- If you are planning to roll out the Viva Connections app experience only for desktop users, you can use the PowerShell approach to prepare a package and upload it as a Teams app.

- If you are planning to roll out the Viva Connections app experience for both desktop and mobile users, you can use the built-in Teams app.

PowerShell for Desktop-Only Experience

In the early days of the Viva Connections release, Microsoft released a PowerShell script to prepare a package for Viva Connections. You should still use this PowerShell approach to enable a desktop-only experience.

The PowerShell script is available to download at the following location:

```
https://www.microsoft.com/download/confirmation.aspx?id=102888
```

Follow these steps to prepare the package:

1. Download and install the latest version of the SharePoint Online Management Shell.

2. Connect to SharePoint Online as a SharePoint administrator or Global administrator.

Figure 8-2 shows PowerShell script execution for preparing a package for Viva Connections desktop-only experience.

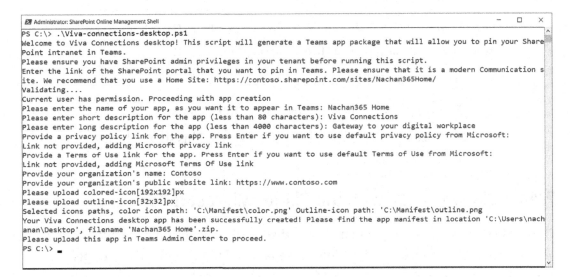

Figure 8-2. *PowerShell to prepare the package*

The script will ask for the following parameters:

- *Home site URL*: Provide the URL of the SharePoint home site that will become a landing experience in Viva Connections.

- *App Name*: Provide the name of your app, as you want it to appear in Microsoft Teams.

- *App short description*: Describe your app (in less than 80 characters), as you want it to appear in Microsoft Teams.

- *App long description*: Describe your app (in less than 4,000 characters), as you want it to appear in Microsoft Teams.

- *Privacy policy link for the app*: Provide a custom Teams app policy link. Leave this empty if you do not have any policy and to use the default SharePoint privacy policy from Microsoft.

- *Terms of use for the app*: Provide the terms of use for the custom Teams app. Leave this empty if you do not have any and want to use the default terms of use from Microsoft.

- *Organization name*: Provide the company name that will be available on the app page as "Created by."

- *Organization website*: Provide the company website URL that will be available on the app page as the company landing page.

- *Icons*: Provide two PNG icons for your app.

  - *192×192 pixels*: Available in the Teams app catalog.

  - *32×32 pixels*: Available in the Teams app bar. This should be a monochrome icon.

Prepare the Package with the CLI for Microsoft 365

The CLI for Microsoft 365 is an open source Microsoft 365 Platform Community (PnP) project that helps manage the Microsoft 365 tenant and build automation scripts. The CLI command m365 viva connections app create helps to create the Viva Connections desktop app package for Microsoft Teams.

The following is an example to create a Viva Connections desktop app package:

```
m365 viva connections app create
--portalUrl https://contoso.sharepoint.com
--appName Contoso
--description "Contoso company app"
--longDescription "Stay on top of what's happening at Contoso"
--companyName Contoso
--companyWebsiteUrl https://contoso.com
--coloredIconPath icon-color.png
--outlineIconPath icon-outline.png
```

More information about the CLI for Microsoft 365 approach can be found at
`https://pnp.github.io/cli-microsoft365/cmd/viva/connections/connections-app-create/`.

Upload the Viva Connections Desktop Package in the Teams Admin Center

The zip package prepared by following any of the previous approaches needs to be uploaded to Microsoft Teams to make it available as an app to the end users.

Follow these steps to upload the package to the Teams Admin Center:

1. Open the Microsoft Teams Admin Center (`https://admin.teams.microsoft.com`).

2. From the left navigation, click Teams apps ➤ Manage apps.

3. Click Upload.

Figure 8-3 shows how to manage apps in the Microsoft Teams Admin Center.

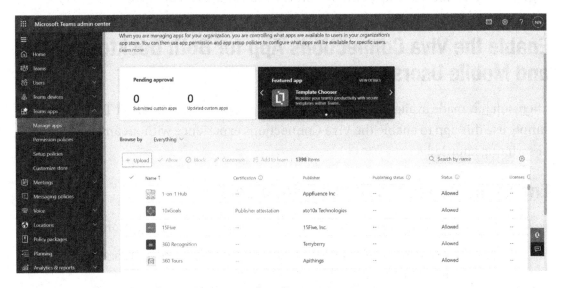

Figure 8-3. *Teams Admin Center, uploading an app*

As shown in Figure 8-4, the Viva Connections desktop app should be enabled and available to configure.

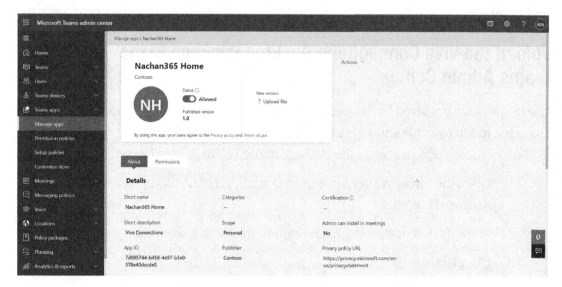

Figure 8-4. Teams Admin Center, Viva Connections desktop app

Enable the Viva Connections App for Both Desktop and Mobile Users

Microsoft has made available the Viva Connections app inside Microsoft Teams. You can simply use this app to enable the Viva Connections experience without any PowerShell or scripting knowledge.

Enable the App in the Teams Admin Center

Follow these steps to enable the Viva Connections app in the Teams Admin Center:

1. Open the Microsoft Teams Admin Center (`https://admin.teams.microsoft.com`).

2. From the left navigation, click Teams apps ➤ Manage apps.

3. In "Search by name," type **Viva Connections**.

Figure 8-5 shows an initial blocked status of the Viva Connections app in the Microsoft Teams Admin Center.

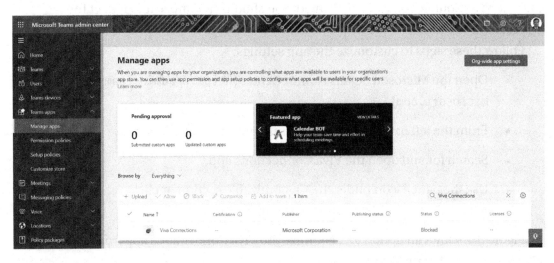

Figure 8-5. *Microsoft Teams Admin Center, searching for the Viva Connections app*

The Viva Connections app is blocked by default. As shown in Figure 8-6, click the app and toggle the status to Allowed. This will enable the Viva Connections app for the organization.

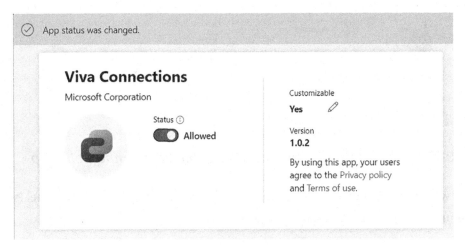

Figure 8-6. *Teams Admin Center, enabling the Viva Connections app*

Customize the App Settings

After the Viva Connections app is enabled, you should customize it to reflect the organization's branding.

Follow these steps to customize the app settings:

- Open the Microsoft Teams Admin Center (`https://admin.teams.microsoft.com`).

- From the left navigation, click Teams apps ➤ Manage apps.

- Search for and open the Viva Connections app.

- Use the pencil icon under the Customizable section or click Actions ➤ Customize to start customizing the app.

Figure 8-7 shows an option to customize the Viva Connections app from the Microsoft Teams Admin Center.

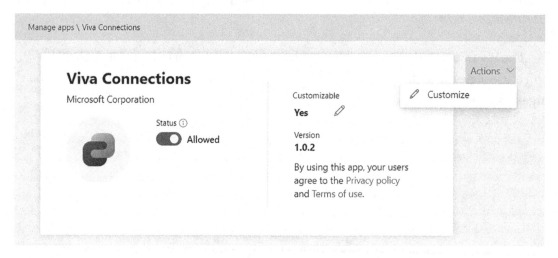

Figure 8-7. *Teams Admin Center, customizing the Viva Connections app*

This will open a panel to set a personalized branding experience. The panel is divided into two sections: Details and Icons.

Details Section

As shown in Figure 8-8, the Details section helps you customize the information of the app when it is available in the Teams app catalog and Teams app bar.

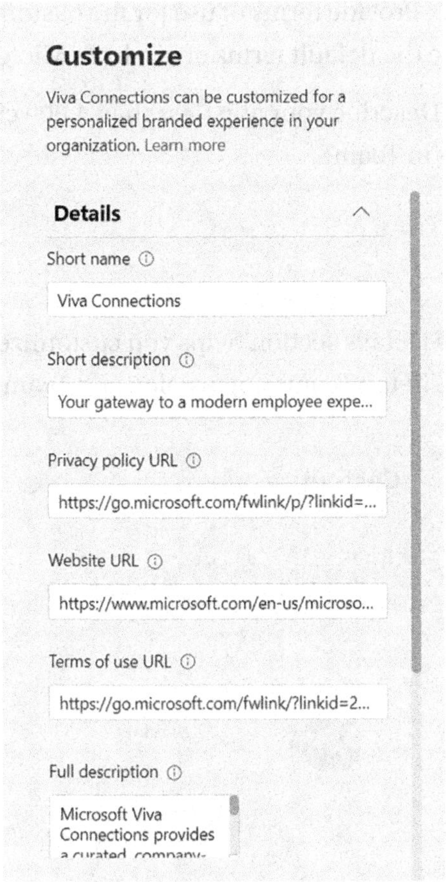

Figure 8-8. *Customizing the Viva Connections app, Details section*

In the Details sections, you can customize the following visual information for the app:

- *Short name*: Provide the name of your app as you want it to appear in Teams.

- *Short description*: Describe your app (less than 80 characters) as you want it to appear in Teams.

- *Privacy policy URL*: Provide the custom teams app policy link. By default, it will use the default SharePoint privacy policy from Microsoft.

- *Website URL*: Provide the company website URL that will be available on the app page as the company landing page.

- *Terms of use URL*: Provide terms of use for the custom Teams app. By
  default, it will use the default terms of use from Microsoft.

- *Full description*: Describe your app (less than 4,000 characters) as you
  want it to appear in Teams.

Icons Section

As shown in Figure 8-9, the Details section helps you customize the visual appearance of
the app when it is available in the Teams app catalog and Teams app bar.

Figure 8-9. *Customizing the Viva Connections app, Icons section*

In the Icons sections, you can customize the following visual appearance of the app:

- *Color icon*: Provide a PNG icon (192×192 pixels) to be available in the Teams app catalog.

- *Outline icon*: Provide a PNG icon (32×32 pixels) to be available in the Teams app bar. This should be a monochrome icon.

- *Accent color*: Choose the color to match your icon background.

Once you customize the app appearance, review the changes under the About ➤ Details section of the app.

Define Policies for the App

Now we have the Viva Connections app ready to use. However, it might not be a good idea to roll it to the entire organization in one go. It is advisable to perform a phased rollout of the app. This will help you to gather feedback from pilot users and make improvements. You will have to decide your pilot users and roll out a plan for them.

To plan it better, you can consider a similar approach to Microsoft, which rolls out its updates by defining rings. Figure 8-10 shows an example of defining a phased rollout plan for Viva Connections.

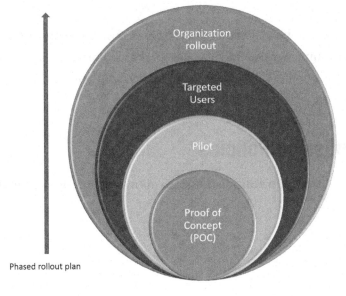

Figure 8-10. *Phased rollout plan*

Defining Your Rings for a Phased Rollout

It is important to identify your target set of users, create a feedback mechanism, and adapt to the changes. The following are the potential rings to define:

- *Proof of concept (POC)*: Target the business users to analyze the value of this exercise and technical experts to carry out the feasibility of the solution.

- *Pilot*: This is a wider group of business analysts and technical experts who can evaluate whether the app meets the end-user expectations before its rollout.

- *Targeted users*: These are early adopters (e.g., champions) identified in your organization who can provide constructive feedback. Making the app available to champions would be about giving them time to prepare before the broader rollout so that they can champion the rollout.

- *Organization rollout*: Once we have the feedback from each ring accepted and worked upon, it is time to roll it out to the entire organization.

We will cover more about educating your users about the Viva Connections app in Chapter 10.

This rollout plan can be achieved by carefully planning the policies in the Teams Admin Center. In simple words, policies enable us to make a feature available to a few users and restrict it for others. We can use the permission policies and setup policies to effectively roll out the Viva Connections app.

Define Permission Policies

The permission policies help administrators to allow or block apps from the Microsoft Teams store.

Follow these steps to add a permission policy to allow the Viva Connections app for a certain set of users and restrict it from others:

1. Open the Microsoft Teams Admin Center (`https://admin.teams.microsoft.com`).

2. From the left navigation, click Teams apps ➤ Permission policies.

3. Click Add to create a new permission policy.

Figure 8-11 highlights an option to monitor and define a permission policy.

Figure 8-11. *Adding a new app permission policy*

Add a new policy by defining values for the following options:

- *Name*: Specify a meaningful name to define this policy. For example, the word *Beta* in the policy name can signify the purpose.

- *Description*: Specify a description of which apps will be available to the users in this policy.

- *Microsoft apps*: Specify the list of allowed apps (e.g., Viva Connections).

Figure 8-12 shows an example of the app permission policy for Viva Connections.

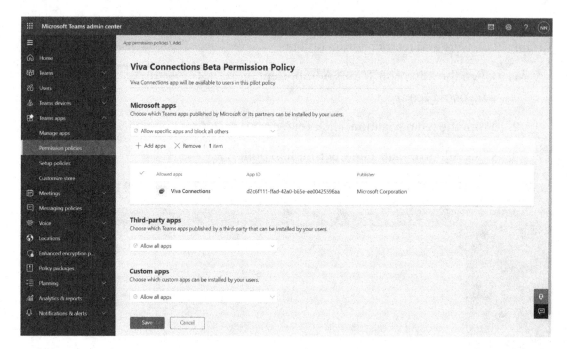

Figure 8-12. App permission policy for Viva Connections

A Real-World Scenario

The configuration might not be as simple as we have defined now. Because with this configuration, users will lose access to all other Microsoft apps as well.

To overcome this problem, you can follow this approach:

1. Modify the Global (Org-wide default) policy to block the Viva Connections app and allow others.

2. Create a new beta policy to allow a specific app, i.e., the Viva Connections app, and block others.

Assign Permission Policy to Users

There are various ways available to assign a permission policy to the users.

Option 1: Permission Policy Interface

Follow these steps to add users to the permission policy:

1. In the Microsoft Teams Admin Center, from the left navigation, click Teams apps ➤ Permission policies.

2. Select the permission policy.

3. Click "Manage users."

4. In the panel, search and add the user to be added to the permission policy.

5. Click Apply.

Figure 8-13 shows an option to add users to the permission policy.

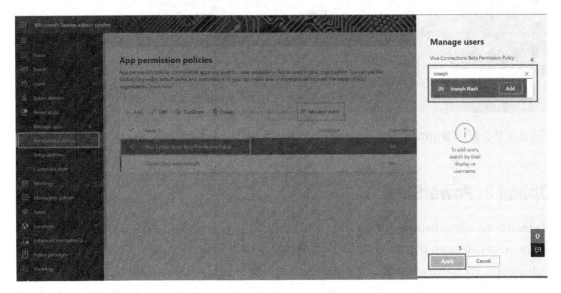

Figure 8-13. *Adding users to the permission policy*

Option 2: Permission Policy Interface

Follow these steps to assign a permission policy to an individual user:

1. In the Microsoft Teams Admin Center, in the left navigation, click Users ➤ Manage users.

2. Select the individual user to assign the policy.

3. Click "Edit settings."

4. Select the policy to assign under the App permission policy.

5. Click Apply.

Figure 8-14 shows an option to assign permission policy to an individual user.

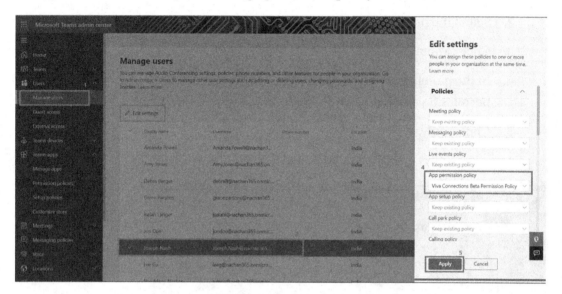

Figure 8-14. *Assigning the permission policy to an individual user*

Option 3: PowerShell

If you are an administrator and want to automate the permission policy assignment for the user, you can use the PowerShell option. The PowerShell option is helpful to automate a scenario of assigning policies to multiple users at the same time.

The prerequisite is to install the Teams PowerShell by running the following command:

```
Install-Module -Name MicrosoftTeams
```

```
Execute below PowerShell cmdlets
```

```
# Connect using Teams PowerShell Module
# Specify the Microsoft Teams administrator credentials to connect
Import-Module MicrosoftTeams
$credential = Get-Credential
Connect-MicrosoftTeams -Credential $credential
```

```
# If you have MFA (Multi-Factor Authentication) enabled, use the
below command
# Connect-MicrosoftTeams -AccountId user@domain.microsoft.com

# Assign permission policy to a user
Grant-CsTeamsAppPermissionPolicy -Identity "Joseph.Nash@contoso.com"
-PolicyName "Viva Connections Beta Permission Policy"
```

Manage Permission Policies with PowerShell

To effectively manage the permission policies and user assignment, you should consider
using PowerShell, as the Teams Admin Center UI provides limited options.

List the App Permission Policies

Use the following PowerShell command to list the app permission policies in a tenant:

```
Get-CsTeamsAppPermissionPolicy
```

Figure 8-15 shows an example of listing the app permission policies.

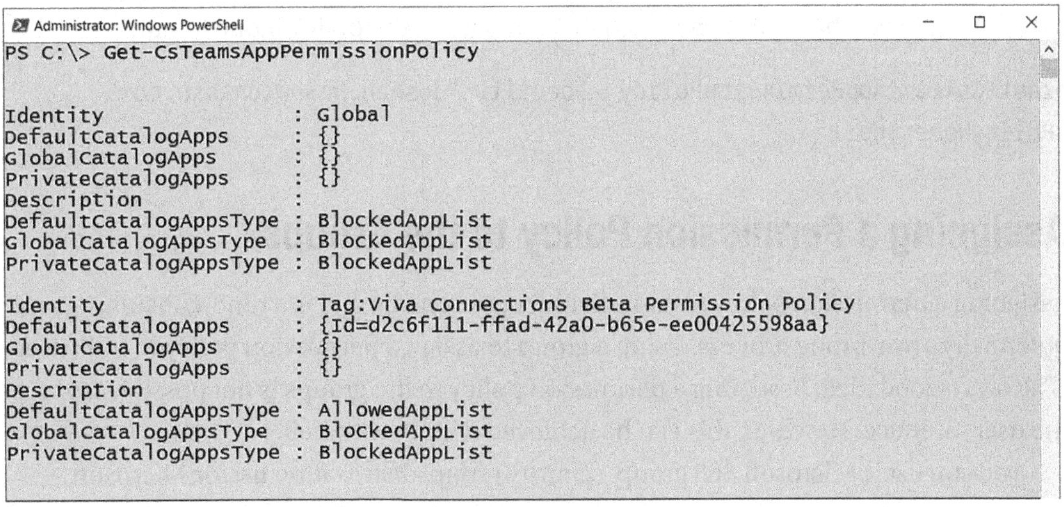

Figure 8-15. Listing the app permission policies

Assign Users to the App Permission Policy

Use the following PowerShell to assign users to the permission policy.

```
$Users = Get-CsOnlineUser | Select-Object DisplayName, SipAddress,
TeamsAppPermissionPolicy
$Users | Where-Object {$_.TeamsAppPermissionPolicy.Name -eq "Viva
Connections Beta Permission Policy" }
```

Figure 8-16 shows an example of listing users assigned to the app permission policy.

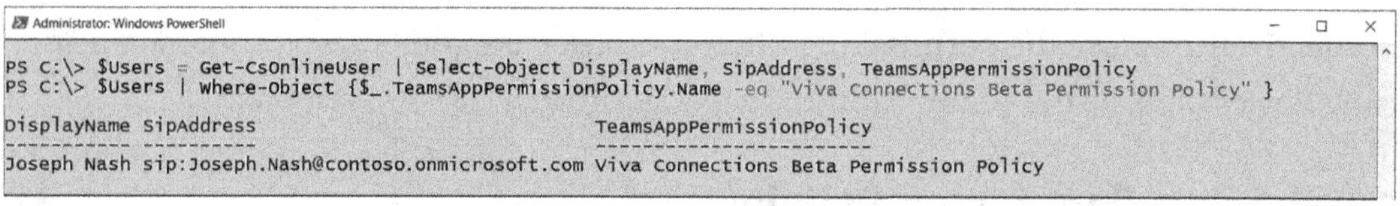

Figure 8-16. *Assigning users to the app permission policy*

Unassigning a Custom Policy of the User

To unassign a custom policy of the user, simply set the policy to Global (Org-wide default). In PowerShell, this can be achieved by setting the policy name to null.

```
Grant-CsTeamsAppPermissionPolicy -Identity "Joseph.Nash@contoso.com"
-PolicyName $null
```

Assigning a Permission Policy to the Groups

Assigning a permission policy to an individual user one by one is a time-consuming and potentially error-prone process. Using a group to assign a permission policy to bulk users is always a good idea. Assigning a permission policy to the groups is not possible from the user interface. However, this can be achieved with PowerShell.

You can use a Microsoft 365 group, security group, distribution list, or Microsoft Teams team for policy assignment. As the members are added or removed from the group, their policy assignment gets updated accordingly.

Assign a Permission Policy to Team Members

To assign a permission policy to members of a Microsoft Teams team, use the following PowerShell command:

```
# Get the Microsoft Teams team
$pilotTeam = Get-Team -DisplayName "Pilot Users"

# Get the team members (including owners)
$teamMembers = Get-TeamUser -GroupId $pilotTeam.GroupId -Role Member

# Assign permission policy to each user
$teamMembers | ForEach-Object { Grant-CsTeamsAppPermissionPolicy
-PolicyName "Viva Connections Beta Permission Policy" -Identity $_.User }
```

Points to Consider

The following are a few points to consider while assigning a permission policy to the users:

1. At a given point in time, a user can be part of only one permission policy.

2. When you assign a permission policy to a user, the user is removed from the previously assigned permission policy.

3. When a user is a member of multiple groups, the highest ranking takes precedence.

4. It might take a few hours to apply the permission policy to the user.

Make the App Available to End Users

Now it is time to make the Viva Connections app available to the end users. Again, it is recommended to follow the phased rollout approach instead of the big bang approach.

An app setup policy helps administrators control the app's installation and its pinning to the app navigation bar as a personal app.

Define the App Setup Policy

Follow these steps to create a custom app setup policy:

1. Open the Microsoft Teams Admin Center (`https://admin.teams.microsoft.com`).

2. From the left navigation, click Teams apps ➤ Setup policies.

3. Click Add to create a new permission policy.

Figure 8-17 shows an option to define the app setup policy.

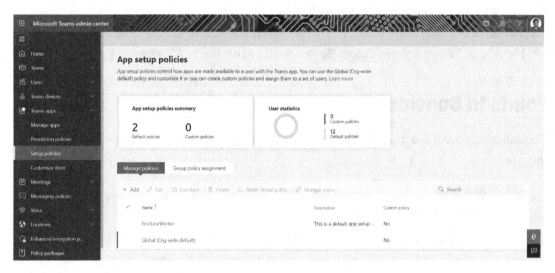

Figure 8-17. *Adding a new app setup policy*

Add a new policy by defining values for the following options:

- *Name*: Specify a meaningful name to define this policy. For example, the word *Beta* in the policy name can signify the purpose.

- *Description*: Specify a description of which apps will be installed and pinned for the users with this policy.

Install the App

To install the Viva Connections app for the users, under Installed apps, click "Add apps." Specify the app installation as follows:

- *Search based on this app permission policy*: Set the scope of the search to apps that are allowed by selecting the permission policy.

- *Apps to add*: Specify the list of allowed apps (e.g., Viva Connections).

Figure 8-18 shows an option to install the Viva Connections app using a setup policy.

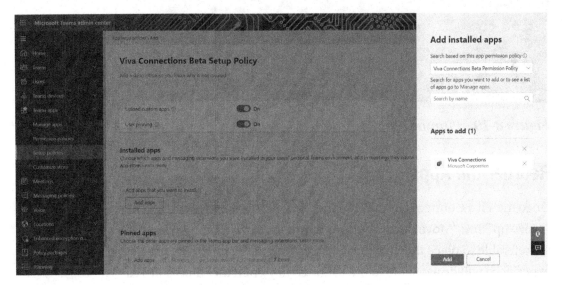

Figure 8-18. *App setup policy for Viva Connections*

Pin the App to the Teams App Bar

Pinning the app to the Teams app bar makes it easy for the users to navigate to the app. You can pin the important apps to the Microsoft Teams app bar and set the order in which they will appear to the users.

Follow these steps to pin the Viva Connections app to the Teams app bar:

1. Open the app policy created in the previous step.

2. Under "Pinned apps," click "Add apps."

3. Search and add the Viva Connections app.

Figure 8-19 shows an option to pin the Viva Connections app to the Teams app bar.

Figure 8-19. *Pinning the Viva Connections app*

Reorder the Apps

Once the Viva Connections app is added, it will be placed at the end of the list. Use the "Move up" and "Move down" buttons to order the Viva Connections app as desired. It is preferable to place the Viva Connections app at the top of the list so that your digital experience will be available to the users as they open the Microsoft Teams.

Figure 8-20 shows an option to reorder the Viva Connections app to the Teams app bar.

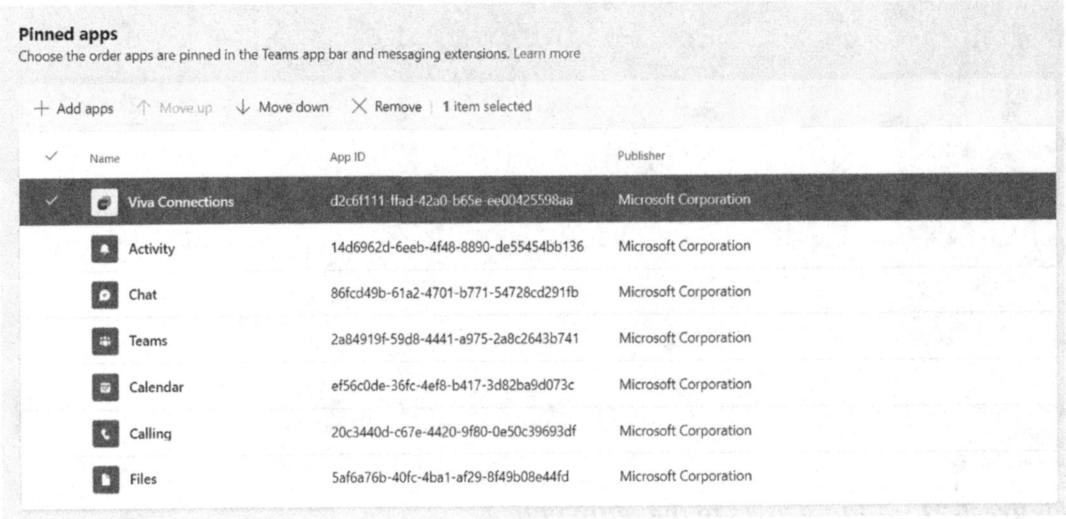

Pinned apps
Choose the order apps are pinned in the Teams app bar and messaging extensions. Learn more

	Name	App ID	Publisher
✓	Viva Connections	d2c6f111-ffad-42a0-b65e-ee00425598aa	Microsoft Corporation
	Activity	14d6962d-6eeb-4f48-8890-de55454bb136	Microsoft Corporation
	Chat	86fcd49b-61a2-4701-b771-54728cd291fb	Microsoft Corporation
	Teams	2a84919f-59d8-4441-a975-2a8c2643b741	Microsoft Corporation
	Calendar	ef56c0de-36fc-4ef8-b417-3d82ba9d073c	Microsoft Corporation
	Calling	20c3440d-c67e-4420-9f80-0e50c39693df	Microsoft Corporation
	Files	5af6a76b-40fc-4ba1-af29-8f49b08e44fd	Microsoft Corporation

Figure 8-20. *Reordering the Viva Connections app*

Assigning a Setup Policy to Users

Follow these steps to add users to the app policy:

1. In the Microsoft Teams Admin Center, from the left navigation, click Teams apps ➤ Setup policies.

2. Select the permission policy.

3. Click "Manage users."

4. In the panel, search and add the user to be added to the app policy.

5. Click Apply.

Figure 8-21 shows an option to add users to the setup policy.

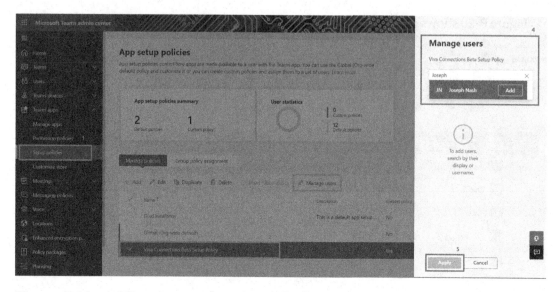

Figure 8-21. *Adding users to the setup policy*

PowerShell Support

You can use the following cmdlet to assign a custom setup policy to the user:

```
Grant-CsTeamsAppSetupPolicy -identity "Joseph.Nash@contoso.com" -PolicyName
"Viva Connections Beta Setup Policy"
```

Assign a Setup Policy to Groups

You can use Microsoft 365 group, security group, distribution list, or Microsoft Teams team for app policy assignment. As the members are added or removed from the group, their policy assignment gets updated accordingly.

The Teams Admin Center UI supports assigning app policy to a group, unlike a permission policy, where one needs to possess some PowerShell skills.

Follow these steps to assign an app policy to the group:

1. In the Microsoft Teams Admin Center, from the left navigation, click Teams apps ➤ Setup policies.

2. Click "Group policy assignment."

3. Click Add.

4. In the panel,

- Search and add the group to be assigned to the app policy.

- Specify the rank; when a user is a member of multiple groups, the highest ranking takes precedence (1 being the highest rank).

- Select the policy.

5. Click Apply.

Figure 8-22 shows an option to assign the setup policy to groups.

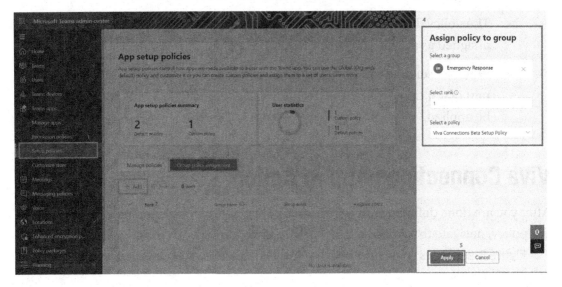

Figure 8-22. *Assigning the setup policy to the group*

PowerShell Support

You can use the following cmdlet to assign a custom setup policy to the group:

```
New-CsGroupPolicyAssignment -GroupId emergencyresponse@contoso.com
-PolicyType TeamsAppSetupPolicy -PolicyName "Viva Connections Beta
Setup Policy"
```

If a user is a member of multiple groups, the policy that has the highest group assignment ranking for the given policy type takes precedence.

Points to Consider

The following are a few points to consider while assigning a setup policy to the users:

- By default, a global (Org-wide default) policy is applied to the user.

- At a given point in time, a user can be part of only one setup policy.

- When you assign a setup policy to a user, the user gets removed from the previously assigned setup policy.

- It might take a few hours to apply the setup policy to the user.

- The policy directly assigned to the user takes precedence over being assigned as part of a group as a member.

- When a user does not have any direct setup policy assigned and is part of multiple groups, the assignment with the highest ranking will be applied.

Viva Connections App in Action

After you are done defining your permission policy, setup policy, and user assignment to the policy, navigate to Microsoft Teams to see Viva Connections in action.

Figure 8-23 shows an example of the Viva Connections app experience in Microsoft Teams.

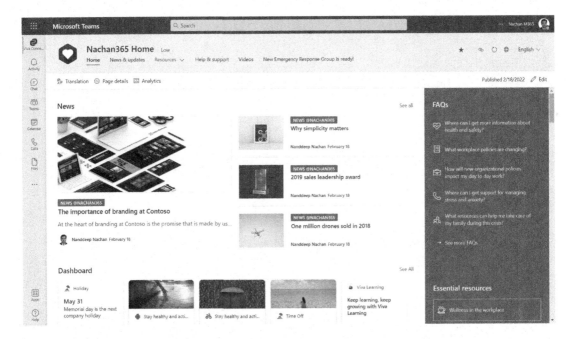

Figure 8-23. *Viva Connections app experience in Microsoft Teams*

Conclusion

You should now have a better understanding of the process to configure the Viva Connections app in Microsoft Teams and to define a rollout strategy. The permission policies help administrators allow or block apps from the Teams store. The app setup policy helps administrators control the app's installation and pin it to the app navigation bar as a personal app.

In the next chapter, we will explore the Viva Connections experience for mobile users.

CHAPTER 9

Define Mobile Settings for Viva Connections

Viva Connections is designed to create an engaging experience for both desktop and mobile users. To meet the usability expectations of both information workers and frontline workers, it is important to define the mobile settings for the Viva Connections app.

In this chapter, you will get guidance on the Viva Connections mobile settings.

Note The dashboard is an important aspect to customize the settings for the Viva Connections mobile app.

Viva Connections Mobile Experience

The mobile experience for Viva Connections is optimized to focus on three major elements, which define the engaging mobile experience for users.

Dashboard

The dashboard displays the dynamic cards for users to take quick actions.

Feed

A feed can generally surface the content relevant to the user from SharePoint, Yammer, and Stream.

Resources

The Resources section in the mobile experience displays the global navigation from SharePoint.

© Nanddeep Sadanand Nachan and Smita Sadanand Nachan 2022
N. S. Nachan and S. S. Nachan, *Up and Running on Microsoft Viva Connections*,
https://doi.org/10.1007/978-1-4842-8606-7_9

Figure 9-1 shows an example of the Dashboard, Feed, and Resources sections of Viva Connections in a mobile experience.

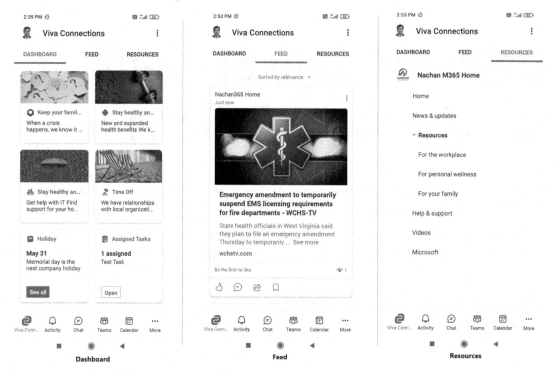

Figure 9-1. *Viva Connections mobile experience*

The feed is an example of a tailored experience, where the content is presented to users based on the communities or sites they follow in SharePoint, group membership in Yammer, or popular content.

The dashboard and resources are examples of a curated experience that can be pushed to users by the site owner or authors. Therefore, it is important to design the dashboard for a mobile experience.

Dashboard for Viva Connections Mobile Experience

While authoring the dashboard and cards on it, it is essential to consider the mobile experience of the dashboard. You can preview the cards in a mobile view to ensure that they are properly displayed. The mobile experience helps you place cards on a screen by clicking "Add a card."

Figure 9-2 shows how to add cards for a mobile view of the dashboard.

Figure 9-2. *Adding a card experience for a mobile view of the dashboard*

The cards on the dashboard can be defined as Medium or Large based on layout. After placing the cards on the dashboard, verify the layout in the mobile experience before publishing.

Figure 9-3 shows an example of cards placed on the dashboard for the mobile view.

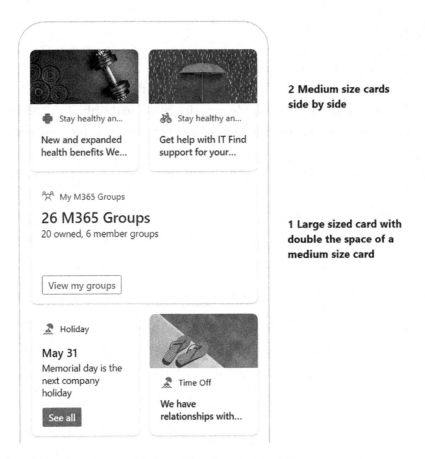

Figure 9-3. *Cards on the dashboard for the mobile view*

Define Settings for the Mobile App

The mobile experience for Viva Connections can be set up after the dashboard is created.

The site administrator or editor on the SharePoint home site can define the mobile experience for the dashboard by placing the cards.

Microsoft Teams administrators can pre-install and pre-pin the Viva Connections app for everyone. The pre-pinned app will automatically appear in the mobile app for Microsoft Teams on Android and iOS.

Pre-installing and pre-pinning the app are optional steps. If not performed, the end users will need to search and install the Viva Connections app as a personal app.

It is important to note that these settings are not specific to the mobile app and when changed apply to both the desktop and mobile experiences.

Conclusion

The mobile experience for Viva Connections is optimized to focus on three major elements: the dashboard, feed, and resources. While authoring the dashboard and cards on it, it is essential to consider the mobile experience of the dashboard. The SharePoint home site administrator or editor and Microsoft Teams administrator can help shape the mobile experience.

In the next chapter, we will how to educate the end users about how to adapt to the Viva Connections experience.

CHAPTER 10

Define End-User Guidance

End-user guidance is the last but crucial stage for the success of Viva Connections. We are now ready from a business and technology point of view to roll out Viva Connections for our Microsoft 365 users. The rollout has been successful when the users adopt the implementation.

In this chapter, you will learn how to make end users comfortable with this new offering and help them quickly adapt to Viva Connections.

Note It is important to convey a message to the end users that your SharePoint intranet is now in Microsoft Teams.

End-User Psychology

Every human is different. Everyone reacts differently to changes. A few end users might be eager to make their move to newer offerings, while you might see pushback from a few end users when adapting to new implementations.

The success of this entire exercise lies in how easily and quickly end users can adapt to this change and start using Viva Connections as their new digital experience.

How Easy or Difficult Is It?

Viva Connections is the integration of SharePoint, Yammer, and Stream with Microsoft Teams. A technical audience with prior experience might feel more at ease knowing that Viva Connections consists of the tools they already use. However, to drive the adoption, it is important to understand the "why" behind the Viva Connections experience.

N. S. Nachan and S. S. Nachan, *Up and Running on Microsoft Viva Connections*, https://doi.org/10.1007/978-1-4842-8606-7_10

The main driver behind adopting Viva Connections for end users is the power it brings by offering information from various sources in a single place in Microsoft Teams. With this change, end users will not need to visit multiple places, including the SharePoint home site, organizational news sites, and Yammer communities, to get updates. Rather, all those updates are at their fingertips, within their comfortable experience of Microsoft Teams, which is now at the center of everyone's digital experience.

Prepare Your Adoption Plan

Every organization has its own culture. Planning for a new tool and helping users adapt to it is always a different journey for every organization. There is no one rigid plan to make it work.

The following are a few considerations that will help you get started with end-user adoption at your organization.

User Engagement

User engagement is the key to the success of Viva Connections adoption. The first step is to analyze the different sets of audiences in the organization. Plan and implement adoption stages and steps for each of them to drive better user engagement at each stage.

Find the Early Adopters

Every organization has enthusiasts who are passionate about technology and like to explore new things, evaluate the functionality, and provide their open constructive feedback.

For the success of Viva Connections, identify the early adopters and draw on their enthusiasm to evaluate the Viva Connections experience.

Organizations should ensure that employees not only get engaged but stay engaged in a sustainable way. Ensure the freshness of the content from various sources including SharePoint, Yammer, and Stream. Place engaging cards on the dashboard to help find information easily. Implement a solid feedback channel for continuous improvement of the Viva Connections experience.

Build a Champions Program

Champions are a specialized role for driving engagements. It is an important role from any organization's perspective because learning with the help of colleagues is considered the most effective method over self-learning or formal training.

Champions can help for the business transformation and easy adoption of changes by creating excitement and influencing others by spreading the word.

Spread Awareness

Start by spreading the word about this new offering and start drawing end-user attention to let them know that something interesting is coming their way.

Identify Channels

Identify the most engaging mediums or channels in the organization that can act as effective communication tools such as SharePoint, Yammer, Microsoft Teams, etc.

Advertise

Based on the identified channels, advertise the new Viva Connections offerings by creating SharePoint news or announcements, Yammer conversations, and Microsoft Teams channel posts.

While posting on these channels, make sure it is not one-way communication; rather, encourage users to participate in the discussions, resolve their queries, and get them excited about the new rollout.

Communications

Create engaging email announcement templates to send emails to users; see `https://adoption.microsoft.com/viva/`. Stick physical posters at the common places including meeting rooms, the cafeteria, etc., to attract users' attention.

Training

Training can help raise awareness about the subject.

Train the End Users

Provide formal training to end users to get them up to speed on using Viva Connections. Record short videos explaining Viva Connections and post them on channels including SharePoint, Yammer, and Microsoft Teams.

Implement Storytelling by Champions

Champions can help bridge the gap between business scenarios and user expectations. Promote channels for champions where they can share success stories and helpful tips to the end users.

Measure the Success

To measure how effectively Viva Connections is being used across the organization, you should define the metrics to measure.

Measure Usage Analytics

Based on the information being presented on the SharePoint home site, as well on the dashboard cards, measure the traffic to those sites.

The following are a few metrics that can be measured:

- *Microsoft 365 usage analytics*: Track the overall usage of apps including SharePoint, Yammer, and Microsoft Teams.

- *SharePoint site or page analytics*: If the SharePoint page is referred to as a link on the dashboard card or SharePoint news is published via the SharePoint home site or an organizational news site, then the user engagement can be tracked via the SharePoint site or page analytics.

- *Yammer analytics*: When a Yammer conversation is featured on the SharePoint home site, its engagement can be tracked with Yammer analytics.

Encourage Feedback

Viva Connections is an employee experience in a digital workplace. It is all about employees and their information. Considering this, encourage direct feedback from your employees by asking these questions:

- What do they like about the experience?

- What do they think is lacking?

- What can be done to improve the experience?

Setting up Microsoft Forms to collect feedback from users is a nice and out-of-the-box option to consider.

Create Forums

Employees might face usability or technical issues while accessing the Microsoft Viva Connections. Encourage employees to submit the issues. Set up Microsoft Teams channels, SharePoint sites, or Yammer communities where they can have a conversation around any issue with the champions. Champions can help them remove the blockers and ensure a smooth experience.

Conclusion

The adoption of Viva Connections by the end users defines the success of the organization. Every human and organizational culture is different. It is essential to build your plan around the adoption of this tool change for your end users.

In the next chapter, we will learn to meet custom business scenarios by extending Viva Connections.

CHAPTER 11

Extending Viva Connections

Microsoft Viva Connections presents a curated experience and insights into the organizational culture to engage employees by bringing together news, announcements, and resources. The dashboard offers a consistent experience across mobile and desktop devices.

In this chapter, we will extend Viva Connections with the SharePoint Framework (SPFx) to meet custom business scenarios. This chapter assumes prior experience with SPFx.

Note SPFx provides extensibility for Viva Connections by implementing web parts, application customizers, and adaptive card extensions.

The Need for Extensibility

The dashboard provides a consistent experience across desktop and mobile devices. The dashboard is authored by placing cards on it. The cards provide a flexible way for employees to get quick updates, keep a list of their tasks, and complete the tasks from a single interface.

Various first-party card types available from Microsoft (including Web link, Assigned tasks, Teams App, Shifts, Approvals, Card designer, etc.) make it easy to present cards to the users. Users can take action on a card to complete their tasks.

The Card designer is a special type of card that offers low-code extensibility to author JSON-based cards with more customization options.

© Nanddeep Sadanand Nachan and Smita Sadanand Nachan 2022
N. S. Nachan and S. S. Nachan, *Up and Running on Microsoft Viva Connections*,
https://doi.org/10.1007/978-1-4842-8606-7_11

Various partners and ISVs have rolled out the experience of cards for IT, HR, finance, employee experiences, and other services, which can be easily plugged into Viva Connections. The names include ServiceNow, WorkDay, Moveworks, Limeade, Tribute, LifeWorks, Talentsoft, StandOut, EdCast, Zebra-Reflexis, BlueYonder, Espressive, and many more.

For organizations looking for an experience beyond what is offered by Microsoft's out-of-the-box cards, as well partner solutions, they can involve IT to build the customized solutions using SPFx. Every organization uses various services and systems that are being used by their employees daily. With a Viva implementation, organizations are looking forward to having all the information in one place, i.e., in Microsoft Teams. Presenting employees with the information they need to work effectively can be achieved by developing custom cards on the dashboard. The dashboard experience can be extended with developer experience.

Extensibility Options with SPFx

Viva Connections is surfacing a modern SharePoint home site in Microsoft Teams. Modern SharePoint supports extensibility with modern web tools. SharePoint Framework is the extensibility model for Viva Connections, Microsoft Teams, and SharePoint.

SharePoint Framework supports platform-agnostic, client-side development for SharePoint using modern web technologies and tools (e.g., NodeJS, NPM, Gulp, TypeScript, Yeoman, Webpack, etc.).

As the Viva Connections desktop experience is built with modern SharePoint pages, it can be extended with the following options:

- *Web parts*: These are HTML widgets. Modern SharePoint supports web parts developed with SPFx.

- *Application customizers*: This SPFx-based approach allows you to inject HTML and JavaScript to predefined locations on the SharePoint page.

- *Adaptive card extensions (ACEs)*: ACEs developed with the SharePoint Framework are implemented as JSON structures, which can be placed on the Viva Connections dashboard.

Tools and Libraries for SPFx

SharePoint Framework v1.13 (and newer) supports extending applications for Viva Connections. To build customizations using SPFx, we need to install modern tools and libraries as follows:

Node.js

Node.js is an open-source JavaScript runtime, used to host and serve JavaScript-based applications. Install Node.js v14 from `https://nodejs.org`.

NPM

This stands for Node Package Manager, which installs modules and their dependencies in the `node_modules` folder.

Gulp

This automates SPFx development and deployment tasks. It performs bundling and minification tasks before each build.

Yeoman

This is a scaffolding tool to generate an SPFx solution and build the required project structure.

Yeoman SPFx Generator

This helps to generate a SharePoint client-side solution project with the needed toolchain and project structure.

Gulp, Yeoman, and Yeoman SPFx Generator can be installed all at once using the following command:

```
npm install gulp-cli yo @microsoft/generator-sharepoint --global
```

TypeScript

This is a superset of JavaScript. SPFx applications are written in TypeScript, which is a strongly typed language.

Visual Studio Code

This is a lightweight IDE for writing code for SPFx solutions.

Extensibility with Web Parts

Web parts built with the SharePoint Framework help to implement widgets to surface SharePoint data with REST APIs and also consume Graph APIs to surface data from Microsoft 365 apps and services. The property pane of the web part allows end users to configure the web part.

Viva Connections web parts work only for the desktop experience.

The following are the scenarios where you might want to build web parts:

- To surface information from SharePoint data (e.g., news, SharePoint lists, document libraries)

- To surface information from Microsoft 365 apps and services (e.g., Microsoft 365 Groups, Yammer, Microsoft Teams, etc.)

- To surface information by consuming web services

Figure 11-1 shows an example of a web part developed with the SharePoint Framework to display the hierarchical information from a SharePoint list.

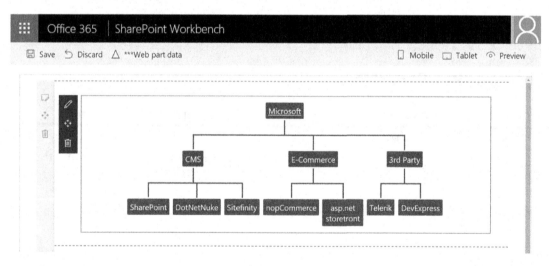

Figure 11-1. *Web part on a SharePoint page*

Extensibility with Application Customizers

Consider building application customizers to extend Viva Connections when you need to add custom code or HTML elements on all the pages in Viva Connections. It is not necessary to have a UI element for the application customizer. You can use an application customizer to run any background code for all pages in Viva Connections.

On a broader term, SPFx extensions allow you to extend the user experience for SharePoint including the notification area, list views, and toolbars.

From the Viva Connections point of view, application customizers are effective to render the custom visualization on the header and footer sections of the page. With application customizers, one can add HTML and JavaScript to a predefined location on the page (e.g., top and bottom sections).

An application customizer can be used to place important notifications or announcements at the top of the page or important links at the bottom of the page. The app bar may affect the customizations that can be achieved using application customizers. Viva Connections application customizers work only for the desktop experience.

Figure 11-2 is an example of an application customizer developed with the SharePoint Framework to show important announcements to the user to help them stay on top of their work.

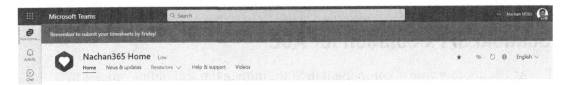

Figure 11-2. *Extensibility with application customizers*

Extensibility with Adaptive Card Extensions

Adaptive card extension (ACE) is a new component type available in the SharePoint Framework to build a rich experience with cards for the dashboard. ACEs use a declarative JSON schema to generate the card UI. When the ACEs are compared with the web part, the main difference is that the web parts can be placed on pages, and developers use web frameworks to implement them. In comparison, ACEs work only on the dashboard and use adaptive cards for the UI. This section is relevant only to developers who are planning to build ACE customizations with the SharePoint Framework.

169

ACEs support the following list of templates:

- Basic card template

- Image card template

- Primary text template

Each card template renders the information differently. Figure 11-3 shows a layout of supported ACE templates.

Basic Card Template   **Image Card Template**   **Primary Text Template**

Figure 11-3. *Supported ACE templates*

Scaffold SPFx Solution for ACE

ACE is another type of component in SPFx. Initiate the scaffolding process by running the following command:

```
yo @microsoft/sharepoint
```

If you have prior experience developing web parts or extensions with the SharePoint Framework, the scaffolding process remains the same. The only difference is to select ACE as the type of client-side component to create. A solution can have multiple ACEs, web parts, and extensions. Figure 11-4 shows Yeoman scaffolding of the SharePoint Framework solution for ACEs.

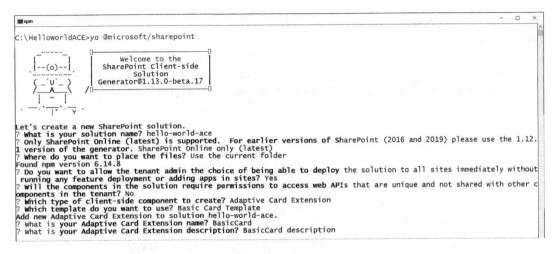

Figure 11-4. *Scaffold ACE solution*

ACE Class (Base Class)

The file src\adaptiveCardExtensions\basicCard\BasicCardAdaptiveCardExtension. ts is the definition of an ACE, which extends from the BaseAdaptiveCardExtension class.

```
export default class BasicCardAdaptiveCardExtension extends
BaseAdaptiveCardExtension<
   IBasicCardAdaptiveCardExtensionProps,
   IBasicCardAdaptiveCardExtensionState
> {
   // ...

}
```

A card view is the view of the card on the dashboard. A quick view is available as a dialog box after acting on the card view.

Each of the card views and quick views must be registered as an identifiable string inside a constructor or onInit() method.

```
public async onInit(): Promise<void> {
...
this.cardNavigator.register(CARD_VIEW_REGISTRY_ID, () => new CardView());
```

171

```
this.quickViewNavigator.register(QUICK_VIEW_REGISTRY_ID, () => new
QuickView());
}
```

Figure 11-5 shows an example of a card view and a quick view.

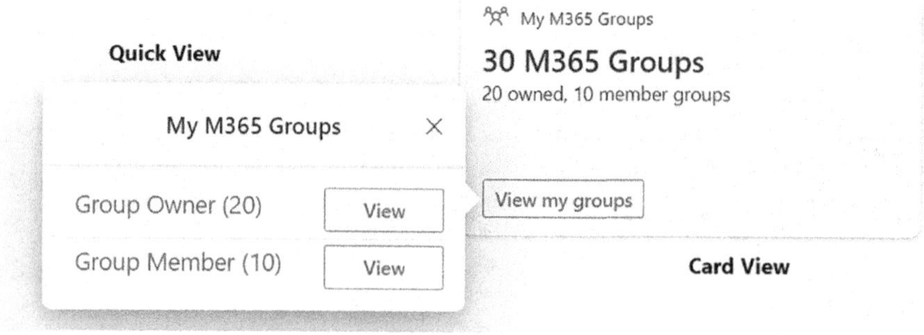

Figure 11-5. *Card view and quick view in action*

Card View

A card view defines the UI and behavior of the card when added to the dashboard.

A card view implementation can be found here:

```
src\adaptiveCardExtensions\basicCard\cardView\CardView.ts
```

The data getter method must be implemented by the card view with a return type unique to the parent class of the view.

```
public get data(): IBasicCardParameters {
    return {
      primaryText: strings.PrimaryText
    };
}
```

The cardButtons property defines the number of buttons on the card and the action to perform.

```
public get cardButtons(): [ICardButton] | [ICardButton, ICardButton] |
undefined {
    return [
      {
```

```
      title: strings.QuickViewButton,
      action: {
        type: 'QuickView',
        parameters: {
          view: QUICK_VIEW_REGISTRY_ID
        }
      }
    },
    {
      title: 'Read more',
      action: {
        type: 'ExternalLink',
        parameters: {
          target: 'https://www.contoso.com'
        }
      }
    }
  ];
}
```

The onCardSelection method defines the behavior when a card is clicked.

```
public get onCardSelection(): IQuickViewCardAction |
IExternalLinkCardAction | undefined {
    return {
        type: 'ExternalLink',
        parameters: {
            target: 'https://www.contoso.com'
        }
    };
}
```

Quick View

The quick view is implemented with JSON templates, which can be seen after acting on the card view actions.

A quick view implementation can be found here:

src\adaptiveCardExtensions\basicCard\quickView\QuickView.ts

The template() getter returns valid adaptive card template JSON for a quick view.

```
public get template(): ISPFxAdaptiveCard {
    return require('./template/QuickViewTemplate.json');
}
```

The quick view JSON contains the bound template slot (for e.g., ${title}, ${description}) as follows:

```
{
  "$schema": "http://adaptivecards.io/schemas/adaptive-card.json",
  "type": "AdaptiveCard",
  "version": "1.2",
  "body": [
    {
      "type": "Container",
      "$data": "${items}",
      "separator": true,
      "items": [
        {
          "type": "TextBlock",
          "text": "${title}",
          "color": "dark",
          "weight": "Bolder",
          "size": "large",
          "wrap": true,
          "maxLines": 1,
          "spacing": "None"
        },
        {
          "type": "TextBlock",
          "text": "${description}",
          "color": "dark",
          "wrap": true,
```

```
        "size": "medium",
        "maxLines": 1,
        "spacing": "None"
      }
    ]
  }
]
}
```

The bound template slots are automatically mapped to properties on the object returned from the data() getter method.

```
public get data(): IQuickViewData {
    return {
        title: strings.Title,
        description: this.properties.description
    };
}
```

Deploy the Solution

Follow these steps to prepare the package (.sppkg) and deploy it to the SharePoint app catalog:

1. Create a solution package by running the following commands:

   - gulp bundle --ship

   - gulp package-solution --ship

2. Upload the generated solution package (.sppkg) to the SharePoint tenant app catalog.

3. Edit the dashboard page on the SharePoint home site.

4. Add the custom ACE to the page.

As shown in Figure 11-6, the ACE will show a card view. Clicking a button will pop out a quick view.

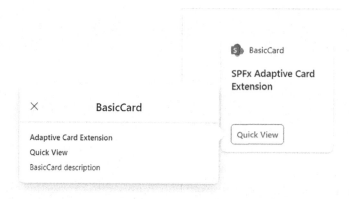

Figure 11-6. *ACE on the dashboard*

For the implementation of ACEs targeting various business scenarios, please refer to the PnP repository for the Viva Connections Viva Adaptive Card (ACE) sample solutions available at `https://github.com/pnp/sp-dev-fx-aces`.

Conclusion

To implement an experience beyond what is offered by the out-of-the-box Microsoft cards, as well partner solutions, you can build customized solutions using the SharePoint Framework. The SharePoint Framework provides extensibility for Viva Connections by implementing web parts, application customizers, and adaptive card extensions.

In the next chapter, you will understand the importance of defining governance for Viva Connections.

CHAPTER 12

Set Up a Governance Strategy

Microsoft Viva Connections brings together knowledge, learning, collaboration, and insights. It helps organizations to modernize the employee experience, stimulate collaboration, and promote the organization's culture. At an organization level, there are multiple stakeholders involved in the life cycle of Viva Connections. It is important to set up a governance strategy so that everything functions smoothly.

In this chapter, you will understand the importance of defining governance for Viva Connections.

Note Governance helps an organization to stay compliant with the processes and regulations.

The Need for Governance

Governance is defined by the set of rules, policies, processes, and responsibilities to deliver the work. Each team in the organization works in partnership to achieve the outcome by following the set governance.

Governance helps organizations to define the vision and answer these questions:

- What defines the key achievements or goals?

- Which tools enable an organization to achieve its goals?

- How do you measure success?

© Nanddeep Sadanand Nachan and Smita Sadanand Nachan 2022
N. S. Nachan and S. S. Nachan, *Up and Running on Microsoft Viva Connections*,
https://doi.org/10.1007/978-1-4842-8606-7_12

The governance plan should evolve as the organization grows and as new capabilities are added to the existing services in Microsoft 365. As Viva Connections is spread across various Microsoft 365 services (e.g., SharePoint, Yammer, Stream, and Microsoft Teams), it is important to identify the roles and responsibilities of individual services, service owners, and collaborators.

These tips will help you ensure you have a well-defined governance policy:

- Every organization has certain policies. Ensure the policies and guidelines for Microsoft 365 do not conflict with the organization-level policies.

- The policies and guidelines should be easily accessible. Place them at a location where users can easily find them.

- Define roles and responsibilities. However, do not make them people-centric. Carry out automation wherever possible (e.g., approvals, autoprovisioning, etc.)

- As the organization and Microsoft 365 evolve, review and revise the policies and guidelines as needed.

Governance for a SharePoint Intranet

Viva Connections surfaces the SharePoint home site in Microsoft Teams. Considering that the SharePoint home site is a digital gateway of the organization, there should be governance set around the site architecture and content.

A governance plan for a SharePoint intranet should involve the following steps:

1. Define the priorities.

2. Prevent the content sprawl.

3. Assign roles and responsibilities.

4. Liaise expectations and define goals.

A governance team should be formed around business stakeholders to reflect on the goals, legal, and advisory board members to ensure processes are followed, and around an IT team to set up the architecture.

To set up governance for a SharePoint intranet, focus on the following key aspects:

- Home site

- Dashboard

- Global navigation and app bar

- Organizational news sites

While planning the governance for the intranet, the following points are worth considering.

Vision

Define a vision statement of what an organization is planning to achieve with the intranet. The vision should define the ownership, which can be shared by more than one entity in an organization. For example, based on the vision of business users, IT should build an intranet.

Information Architecture

Set up governance for the information architecture for defining content, navigation, and site structure. Define content types, metadata, and labels for the content. Promote the flat hierarchy architecture for sites. Define different levels of architecture including global, hub, and local.

- *Navigation*: Define how users can navigate the content by defining links to important resources.

- *Page structure*: Define guidelines for pages, sections, and layout of content for a consistent experience.

- *Metadata*: Define guidelines for metadata, columns, and content types to support organizing the content better.

- *Search*: Understand the search requirement of users and define how they can discover the content.

Policies

Policies define guidelines or recommendations that cover content, design, security, branding, etc. For example, a site should have at least two owners. Each site should have a label specified.

A policy should broadly cover the following points:

- Site designs for consistent look and feel

- Site navigation

- Naming conventions for site, lists, and files

- Sharing capabilities

- Metadata

- Enterprise content types

Site Creation

Define governance on who can create a site in SharePoint and what the approval process should be to request the site. The site creation option should not be open to all, because if there are a large number of sites that get created without governance with loads of content, the important content may get lost in the search experience, and it will rise to a content sprawl issue.

Navigation and Search

By nature, end users navigate first before searching for the content. Well-defined governance for navigation and information architecture makes a consistent experience for users to navigate. Improve the search experience for the users by using search features like acronyms, bookmarks, locations, Q&A, floor plans, etc.

Branding

Define the organization's look and feel by creating organization-specific branding with site scripts and site designs. Site themes will help to have a consistent visual experience in the intranet.

Branding should broadly cover the following points:

- Define branding standards for the organization.

- Define how compliant images are used in content creation.

- Design organizational assets library for content creators.

- Define how accessibility standards are followed on the content.

Content Management

Managing content is an important part of the intranet. Better managed content creates a better navigation and search experience for end users.

A governance plan around the following key points will help you manage the content better on the intranet:

- *Content creation*:

    - Who owns the content? The content creation should not be the responsibility of IT but the communications team or business stakeholders instead.

    - What content should and should not be published?

    - What resources should be made available for content creation (e.g., images, logos, style guidelines, etc.)?

    - Define how sensitive information can be protected.

    - Define how the content should be positioned.

    - Define how to schedule content availability.

    - Define a scheduling window.

    - Define the guidelines for content creation.

    - Follow accessibility standards.

    - Define naming conventions.

- *Information protection*:

    - Define sensitivity labels for your content.

    - Define retention policies.

- *Content rieview*:

  - Define a process to review the content before it is published.

  - For multilingual scenarios, assign content reviewers for each supported language.

  - Define the roles and responsibilities for content review.

- *Policies*:

  - Define policies for content retention and deletion.

Custom Development and Deployment

To design a customized experience, an organization often needs to develop custom solutions with the help of IT. Define standards for the management of development and custom code and the deployment schedules.

Feedback

An intranet should not be a one-way communication. It should also encourage end users to involve and submit their feedback. Build a process to gather and process the feedback from end users (e.g., polls and surveys). Define an owner of feedback. Conduct regular surveys to get the user sentiments for intranet use.

Training

Provide formal training to end users to get them up to speed on using Viva Connections. Record short videos explaining Viva Connections and post them on channels including SharePoint, Yammer, and Microsoft Teams. Incorporate governance policies as part of the training. Consider building a dedicated site for training and related content. Design the role-based pieces of training for site owners, end users, and other groups.

Measure the Success

To measure how effectively Viva Connections and the SharePoint intranet are being used across the organization, you should define the metrics to measure. The following are a few metrics that can be measured:

- Microsoft 365 usage analytics

- SharePoint site or page analytics

- SharePoint Admin Center usage reports

Governance Checklist for Home Site

Based on the organization's culture and business priorities, an organization can define its home site as an intranet. The following governance checklist will help you get started:

- Identify which content should be on the home page.

- Define how the content should be organized.

- Identify who can see which content (audience targeting).

- Define who will update the content.

- Define how often the content should be updated.

- Define which links should be part of the global navigation.

- Define the cards for a better user experience.

- Define which sites should be promoted as organizational news sites.

- Determine who can post on the news site and how often.

- Define who will monitor the performance and other issues.

Stay on Top of Changes

Microsoft 365 development is moving at a rapid pace. Organizations need to adapt to this pace of enhanced features and upcoming changes to services in Microsoft 365. IT always finds it challenging to stay on top of these changes. The Microsoft 365 Roadmap and message center in Microsoft 365 should help IT to stay updated.

Microsoft 365 Roadmap

Microsoft has a public website (https://www.microsoft.com/microsoft-365/roadmap) dedicated to showcasing a roadmap for updates related to Microsoft 365 services.

The IT team can keep themselves updated with the updates in the following stages:

- *In development*: These updates are currently under development and being testing.

- *Rolling out*: Microsoft has started rolling out the features to the tenants, but they are not yet available to all the tenants.

- *Launched*: These features are generally available (GA).

Looking at the upcoming roadmap, the IT team can decide to get the organization prepared for the new enhancements and updates.

Figure 12-1 shows an example of the Microsoft 365 roadmap items.

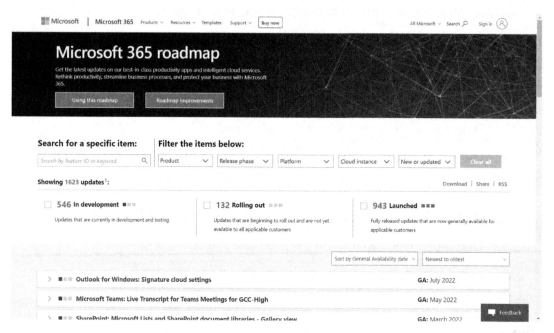

Figure 12-1. *Microsoft 365 roadmap*

Message Center in Microsoft 365

The message center provides a consolidated report of upcoming changes, new and updated features, planned maintenance, and other important updates for all the Microsoft 365 services.

Follow these steps to access the message center:

1. Open the Microsoft 365 Admin Center.

2. Under Health, click "Message center."

Figure 12-2 shows an example of the message center experience in Microsoft 365 where you can get updates on Microsoft 365 services.

Figure 12-2. *Message center*

Conclusion

It is important to set up a governance strategy for a smooth organizational process. Governance should be planned as the first step to stay compliant with the organizational processes and regulations. Governance is an ongoing process. As the organization and Microsoft 365 evolve, review and revise the policies and guidelines as needed.

We wish you the best of luck with setting up and managing Viva Connections at your organization to help everyone build a better workplace!

Index

A

Adaptive card extension (ACE)
    card view, 172, 173
    class, 171, 172
    component type, 169
    quick view, 173–175
    scaffold SPFx solution, 166, 170, 171
    solution, 175, 176
    supported templates, 170
Adoption planning
    awareness spreading, 161
    measuring success, 162, 163
    tool and helping users, 160
    training, 161, 162
    user engagement, 160, 161
Advertising, 161
App bar, 22, 57
    global navigation, 57
    Microsoft Graph, 71
    minimum of read permission, 71
    on modern SharePoint, 71
    My Lists, 57
    SharePoint (*see* SharePoint app bar)
    Viva Connections app, 71, 72
Application customizers, 166, 169
Assigning permission policy, 140–142,
    144, 145

B

Branding, 20, 28, 180–181

C

Card designer, 87–92, 95, 165
Champions program, 161
CLI, Microsoft 365, 130, 131
Collaboration, 29
Communication site, 37, 39, 54, 108
Communication tools, 161
Content creation, 181
Content creator, 106, 107
Content feeds
    chronological approach, 105
    content creator, 106, 107
    content promotion, 106
    desktop experience, 101
    factors, 100
    Feed for Viva Connections, 102
    mobile experience, 100, 101
    ranking, 105
    refreshed content, 105
    SharePoint (*see* Feeds from
        SharePoint)
    sources, 103
    Stream, 104
    user actions on the feed, 106
    user's access, 103
    Yammer, 104
Content management, 181, 182
Coordinated Universal Time (UTC), 52,
    113, 118
Curated experience, 20, 72, 156
Custom app setup policy, 146

© Nanddeep Sadanand Nachan and Smita Sadanand Nachan 2022
N. S. Nachan and S. S. Nachan, *Up and Running on Microsoft Viva Connections*,
https://doi.org/10.1007/978-1-4842-8606-7

D

Dashboard, 13, 22, 155, 165
  addition of cards, 78
    Approvals app, 86, 87
    assigned tasks, 82, 83
    built-in cards, 79
    Card designer card, 87–90
    desktop view, 79
    mobile view, 79
    quick view layout and
      data, 91
    Shifts card, 85, 86
    Teams app, 84
    Top News link card, 87
    web link card, 80
  cards, 73, 76
  connected with organization
    resources, 74
  custom development, 95
  desktop experience, 75
  as a digital toolset, 73
  elements, 75
  employee dashboard (*see* Employee
    dashboard with cards)
  exploration, 75
  layout, 76
  mobile experience, 74
  multilingual support, 78
  partner solutions, 93, 94
  preview and publish
    dashboard, 92, 93
  setting, Viva Connections, 76, 77
  SharePoint communication
    site, 76
  translation, 78
  web view, 76
Data JSON, 91

E

Early adopters, 138, 160
Email announcement, 161
Employee dashboard with cards, 96
  benefits and pay structure, 97
  facilities, 97
  IT support team track
    requests, 97
  user engagement, 96
Employee experience platform (EXP)
  digital platform, 4
  organization, 4, 5
End-user guidance, 24, 159
End-user psychology, 159, 160
Extensibility
  ACE, 169–176
  application customizers, 169
  SPFx, 166, 176
  web parts, 168
External sharing, 31

F

Face-to-face meeting, 3
Feedback, 137, 138, 163, 182
Feed content, *see* Content feeds
Feeds, 15, 23, 99, 104, 155
Feeds from SharePoint
  designation, 107
  experience engagement for the
    users, 108
  insights and analysis, 112, 113
  lookbook templates available for
    news, 108
  news boost feature, 111
  organization's news site, 107
First-party card types, 165

Flat architecture, 31
Flat hierarchy, 29, 31

G

Get-CsTeamsAppPermissionPolicy, 143
Global navigation, 14, 19, 38, 40, 59
  configuration, 61
    logo, 61, 62
    menu item, properties, 64
    navigation source, 62, 63
    title field, 62
  experience of SharePoint, 59
  governance checklist, 66
  home site, 59
  multilingual support, 65
  prerequisites, 60
  setting, 60
  settings menu, 60
  in SharePoint, 59
  Viva Connections experience, 59
Governance
  checklist, 183
  definition, 177
  organizational processes and
      regulations, 185
  plan, 178
  SharePoint intranet, 178–183
Gulp, 167

H

Home site, 54, 55
Home site superpowers
  business and stakeholders, 37
  employee-centric, 38
  employee engagement, 41
  high-traffic sites, 46

home site set up, 39
landing experience, 46
launch, 46
navigation, 38
plan for shaping, 37
PowerShell, 45
security groups, 38
steps, 41
superpowers, 38
Hub sites, 27, 30
Human and organizational culture, 163
Hybrid working, 1, 2, 5, 10
  benefits, 2
  challenges, 3
  employees, 2

I

Information architecture, 26, 27, 179
Information protection, 181

J, K

JavaScript. SPFx applications, 167

L

Landing template, 44

M

Managing permission policies, 143, 144
Medium /Large dashboard, 157
Message center, 185
Metadata, 179
Microsoft's out-of-the-box cards, 95, 166
Microsoft Stream, 120
  built on SharePoint, 121

Microsoft Stream (*cont.*)
    Classic, 120
    migration, 121
Microsoft 365 development, 183
Microsoft 365 Platform Community (PnP)
        project, 130
Microsoft 365 Roadmap, 183, 184
Microsoft 365 services, 178
Microsoft 365 usage analytics, 162
Microsoft Viva, 1, 3–5, 10, 11
    connections, 5, 6, 11, 13, 15, 17, 19, 72
    insights, 6, 7
    learning, 9
    topics, 7, 8
Modern SharePoint search, 29
Modern SharePoint team, 32

N

Navigation, 27–28, 38, 179
Nested hierarchy, 31
News web part, 108–110
Node.js is, 167
Node Package Manager (NPM), 167

O

Official source, 39
onCardSelection method, 173
Organizational news site, 67, 107, 108
Organization rollout, 138

P, Q, R

Page Diagnostics for SharePoint Tool, 46
Page structure, 179
Permission policies, 138–140
Permission policy interface, 141
Phased rollout plan, 137, 138

Pilot, 138
PnP PowerShell, 33
PowerShell
    app enabling, TAC, 132, 133
    CLI for Microsoft 365, 130, 131
    desktop-only experience, 128, 129
    package preparing, 129
    package upload, TAC, 131, 132
    script parameters, 128, 129
    Viva Connections experience, 132
Proof of concept (POC), 138
Public CDN, 48

S

Search user experience, 40
SharePoint, 22, 23, 28, 155, 156, 158
SharePoint Admin Center, 42
SharePoint administrators, 108
SharePoint app bar, 57, 58
    disabled temporarily, 70
    global navigation (*see* Global
        navigation)
    My Files features, 68, 69
    My Lists features, 69, 70
    My News features, 67, 68
    My Sites features, 67
SharePoint communication site, 42
SharePoint experience, 32
SharePoint Framework (SPFx), 18, 33
    extensibility, 166
    modern tools and libraries, 167, 168
SharePoint home site, 35, 36, 38, 54, 57
SharePoint intranet, 25, 33
    branding, 180
    business stakeholders, 178
    collaboration, 26
    custom development and
        deployment, 182

digital workplace, 25
feedback, 182
governance plan, 178
information architecture, 26, 179
key aspects, 179
managing content, 181, 182
navigation and search, 180
organizations, 25, 26
performance, 29
policies, 180
read-only information, 25
site creation, 180
stakeholder, 26
success management, 183
training, 182
vision, 179
SharePoint lookbook, 43
SharePoint Modernization
       scanner, 32
SharePoint page analytics, 113
SharePoint site/page analytics, 162
SharePoint sites, 30, 32, 40
SharePoint start page, 39, 61
SharePoint supports, 28, 29
Site launch, 49
Site launch scheduler, 48
Site launch summary, 52
Site performance, 47
Site usage analytics, 53
Stakeholders engagement, 37

T

Targeted users, 138
Teams Admin Center (TAC), 128, 131
Teams app card, 84
Template JSON, 91
Training, 161, 162, 182

U

Usage analytics, 162
User engagement, 38, 96, 112, 160, 161

V

Video news links, 121, 122, 124
Visual Studio Code, 168
Viva Connections, 5, 11, 15, 19, 71, 72
       app bar, 102
       assigning setup policy, 149–151
       branding, 20
       dashboard, 17, 73, 74, *See also*
              Dashboard
       desktop and mobile users, 132
       employees, 13
       end user availability, 145–152
       experience in Microsoft Teams,
              152, 153
       feeds, 15, 16, 99
       installing, 147
       intranet content, 15
       intranet experience, 14
       localization, 20
       menu, 76
       mobile experience, 17
       organizations, 12
       pinning, 147, 148
       policy definition, 137–145
       PowerShell, 128
       setting customization, 134–137
       setting up, 21
       TAC, 128
Viva Connections experience
       dashboard, 156, 157
       elements, 158
       mobile experience, 18, 155, 156
       mobile setting, 158

Viva Insights module, 4, 6
Viva Learning module, 3
Viva Sales, 10

W, X

Waves, 49, 51
Web link card, 80–82
Web parts, 38, 44, 166, 168, 170

Y, Z

Yammer, 159
    active people in community, 118

analytics, 162
community, 114, 116, 117
conversations, 114
Feature Conversation option, 115, 116
insights, 117, 118
    active members and
      nonmembers, 119
    active people in community,
      118, 119
    content insights, 120
message engagement, 114
organization's Facebook, 114
Yeoman, 167
Yeoman SPFx Generator, 167